I'M NOT WEARING PANTS

True Tales from Canadian Radio Gals

compiled by Kelsi Jordan
www.theradiogirl.com

Cover Design, Interior Design and Page Layout: by Kelsi Jordan and Doug Grelowski of DAT Media (datmedia.ca) Calgary, Alberta

Note for Librarians: A cataloguing record for this book is available from Library and Archives Canada at www.collectionscanada.ca/amicus/index-e.html
ISBN 1-4120-9637-5

Printed in Victoria, BC, Canada. Printed on paper with minimum 30% recycled fibre. Trafford's print shop runs on "green energy" from solar, wind and other environmentally-friendly power sources.

TRAFFORD PUBLISHING™
Offices in Canada, USA, Ireland and UK

Book sales for North America and international:
Trafford Publishing, 6E–2333 Government St.,
Victoria, BC V8T 4P4 CANADA
phone 250 383 6864 (toll-free 1 888 232 4444)
fax 250 383 6804; email to orders@trafford.com
Book sales in Europe:
Trafford Publishing (UK) Limited, 9 Park End Street, 2nd Floor
Oxford, UK OX1 1HH UNITED KINGDOM
phone +44 (0)1865 722 113 (local rate 0845 230 9601)
facsimile +44 (0)1865 722 868; info.uk@trafford.com
Order online at:
trafford.com/06-1393

10 9 8 7 6 5 4 3

Acknowledgments

A huge special THANKS to all the radio gals who submitted their stories. In alphabetical order: Alison Maclean, Amber Lee Trudeau, Andrea Dunn, Andrea Everitt (Shigemi), Cara Graham, Carol Gass, Carol Thomson, Charlee Morgan, Cheryl Brooks, Cristy Beggs, Crystal Lilly, Dee (Diane Jaroway), Denyse Sibley, Eileen Bell, Erin Davis, Jackie Rae Greening, Jodi Hughes, Joy Metcalfe, Kacey Wilson, Karen Daniels, Kelly Grant, Laura Zaina, Laurie Healy, Leanne Cater, Lexine Stephens, Lianne Young, Lisa Cameron, Lisa Rendall, Melanie Risdon, Melissa Wright, Michelle Boden, Natasha Rapchuk, Pam Stevens, Race, Sam Cook, Sandra Plagakis, Sandy Sharkey, Shelby Grayson, Sue Deyell, Sue Stewart, Susan Sierra, Tammy Cole, Tara Dawn Winstone, Tara Holmes and Tish Iceton. You all make me proud to be in radio.

Extra hugs, kisses and high fives to my pals Doug, Lorene, Laurie, Lex, Lindsay and my best bud Lisa.

And a big Ripe Arms to Roger. The landslide will never bring you down.

For Mooch and Peanut

And anyone who has ever been touched by breast cancer

Table of Contents

SANDY SHARKEY

93.9 BOB FM OTTAWA, ONTARIO
WWW.939BOBFM.COM

Sandy Sharkey loves Ottawa and has spent her entire radio career in our nations' capital. She began in 1980 as a commercial copywriter, and today Sandy is the morning show co-host at 93.9 BOB FM.

Sandy has a huge list of memorable radio highlights: the most rewarding happened in 2003, when Sandy was invited on a World Vision trip to the Honduras. She had the amazing opportunity to help 2700 children find sponsors in Ottawa.

Radio has provided Sandy with tons of other cool adventures: she shared a hot tub with Bruce Springsteen at a hotel in Toronto; she was a contestant on "Wheel of Fortune" and won a jet ski; she also interviewed funny man Mike Myers when 'Austin Powers' first hit theatres.

And Sandy's radio career has allowed her to branch out into other areas, like acting. Sandy actually snuck into a closed Rolling Stones video shoot in an Ottawa bar. If you check out the video for 'Streets of Love', you'll see Sandy's fist shaking in the air for at least a second or two.

U2 CAN DO IT

December 2004. I was listening to the U2 cd 'How to Dismantle an Atomic Bomb' when I suddenly realized that it had been almost 25 years since U2 had played a concert in my hometown of Ottawa. I decided right then and there to start an on-line petition.

We HAD to get the band to include us on their upcoming tour.

I co-host 'The Morning After' show on 93.9 BOB FM, which means I talk to thousands of people every morning. Here was my big chance to get all our listeners to sign a 'Bring U2 to Ottawa' petition.

The next morning on the air I shared my big idea with JR, our morning guy. He thought this whole thing was pretty amusing and he didn't hesitate to point out that so far there were only two names on my big petition – my loyal husbands and mine. By the end of the show that morning I had a solid 11 signatures.

I was going to forget the whole thing, but suddenly I had a brainstorm. I would ask the Prime Minister (at the time Paul Martin) to call up his good friend Bono, and request that U2 play in Ottawa.

Paul Martin's friendship with Bono was common knowledge. Bono's efforts to increase foreign aid landed him in the offices of leaders all over the world, and Paul Martin was no exception.

So I called the Prime Minister's office. Every day. Sometimes twice a day. BOB FM listeners continued to sign the petition, and I kept leaving the PM phone messages.

On day 27, I actually reached someone in the Prime Minister's Office. His name was Marc and he thought my idea was hilarious. I'm just glad he had a sense of humour.

"Let me get this straight," he repeated. "You want me to leave a message for our Prime Minister to personally call Bono and persuade him to include Ottawa on U2's tour?"

"Yep," I said. "Think he'll do it?"

On February 15th 2005, Prime Minister Paul Martin called our morning radio show on BOB FM. The fact that he even called made us a little cocky, so we offered him a deal: If Mr. Martin could bring U2 to Ottawa, we would change the name of our radio station to PAUL FM, for one full day.

The Prime Minister was warm and witty. He had a great big laugh but told us that he didn't think it would be a good idea for him to use his position as the leader of our country, to bring a rock band to town.

Well. When you put it that way...

We thanked him for his time and for being so gracious. It was worth a try. Meanwhile our BOB FM listeners were still signing the petition and we had thousands of names. I delivered the petition to Parliament Hill, but didn't have much hope that U2 would ever hear about it.

Which is why Iwas totally shocked a few weeks later. I was having lunch with a friend when I received a call from U2's tour manager.

He wanted me to be the first to know: Bono and Prime Minister Paul Martin had chatted earlier in the week about important humanitarian issues. And before the end of the phone call, Paul Martin mentioned BOB FM's drive to bring U2 here. Bono said "YES" immediately!

After a 25 year absence, U2 was actually including Ottawa on their 'Vertigo' tour! The date of the show would be November 25th.

I couldn't believe it. What started out as a very

tongue-in-cheek thing to keep us amused during the dreary months of winter, turned into something huge. Prime Minister Paul Martin himself joined our morning show on St. Paddy's Day to make the big announcement. And for that one day, BOB FM was officially known as PAUL FM.

Almost a year after we started this crazy idea, U2 came to town. It was the best concert of all time. At least the best concert in 25 years.

And up next ...The Who haven't played Ottawa in ...how long? 30 years? Hmm.

I wonder if Stephen Harper knows Roger Daltrey...

CHARLEE MORGAN

LITE 96 CALGARY, ALBERTA
WWW.LITE96.CA
ALSO HEARD ON **WWW.102CLEARFM.COM**

Charlee was your typical rebellious teenager, always locked in her bedroom listening to music. In 1982, she won a contest to "Be A D.J. For An Hour" on Vancouver radio station CFOX, and since that day she's been hooked on radio.

After high school Charlee enrolled in Broadcasting at B.C.I.T, and got her first radio job in 1985. She has worked at CHAB Moose Jaw, 620 CKCK Regina, Hot Hits LG73 and Kiss FM Vancouver, Lite 96 Calgary and 102.3 Clear FM in Winnipeg.

Charlee has voiced tons of tv and radio commercials. And when she's not busy chatting on-air, she's chatting up 'support' for local youth and animal organizations. Charlee is very committed to her community, and feels incredibly fortunate to still be doing what she loves - talking on air and playing great music.

In her words: "I'll do it until they wheel me out of the control room. In my golden years I'll get a job at the 'Golden Arch's drive through. I'll be on the microphone saying "Welcome to McDonalds, may I take your order please?"

"RICE AND SOME WATER, PLEASE..."

For me, the best part about radio has been the incredible journey. And the wonderful people I've met along the way.

The year was 1985. I had just finished the two-year Broadcast Communications program at B.C.I.T. I was 21 and on my way to Moose Jaw, Saskatchewan for my first 'real' job in radio. I could hardly believe I was going to get paid for doing my two favorite things - talking and playing loud music.

You may have heard the rumor that radio announcers don't make a lot of money. It's NOT a rumor. Especially the first few years. Back in 1985, $800 a month sounded like a lot of money to a naive radio rookie like myself. But moments after receiving my first paycheck, I realized my take home pay was closer to $500 a month. After paying my rent and other bills, I had almost nothing left. I could barely afford to eat. So much for radio being glamorous.

Fortunately I didn't need a car that first year in Moose Jaw. I lived only a block away from the radio station in a suite on top of The Cornerstone Inn and Pub.

Next to my little 2nd floor apartment on Main Street was this great Chinese restaurant where you could get a huge bowl of rice for 50 cents. I quickly became a regular, ordering my usual "rice and water please". Even with the tip my meal was less than a dollar. And Betty, the waitress, was really sweet.

In fact it didn't take long for Betty to become my 'orphan mom." She understood I was far away from all my family and friends, tackling my first 'grown up' job out on my own in a city where I really didn't know anyone. Over time Betty gave me her friendship and on one particular day that I will never forget, she taught me a lesson that stays with me to this day.

It was a few months into my new job. I went into the restaurant to order my usual, "rice and some water, please". Minutes later Betty returned with a heaping hot dish of food. Real food. Tons of it!

"I didn't order this Betty," I said.

"I can't afford this Betty," was what I actually meant. But she already knew that. At that very moment I learned that in 1985 in Moose Jaw, Saskatchewan, people took care of each other. Especially a rookie radio announcer far away from home.

Betty and I have a special bond to this day.

And of course, I think of her every time I see a bowl of rice.

ALI MACLEAN

96.3 JOE FM KINGSTON, ONTARIO
WWW.963JOEFM.COM

Ali's radio career began in Brockville, Ontario at the station she listened to as a teenager - 103.7 The River, 'where Classic Rock Rolls On'. Over the past 12 years Ali has worked in three cities: Brockville, Niagara Falls and now Kingston, Ontario where she is co-host of the morning show at 96.3 JOE FM.

Ali's career highlights include meeting a long list of celebrities. Among her favourites: Steven Tyler from Aerosmith, Harry Connick Jr., Doug Gilmour, Dan Aykroyd, the Tragically Hip and Jason Priestly.

"...ZZZ...ZZZ...ZZZ..."

No matter what career path you choose, you have to start somewhere. In radio, the first few years are the hardest, the most embarrassing, and definitely the most fun.

I'll never forget my first real radio job in the summer of '97. I was doing a bit of everything around the station. During the day I was on the Sea Doo Wave Patrol team ...not much of a team really, just me and another guy. But we actually got paid to ride around on a pair of Sea Doo's and take listeners for rides on the St. Lawrence River. I had a blast that summer. And a wicked tan!

That first radio job also included doing the overnight show from 11pm until 6am. So after a long day out on the water, playing in the sunshine, I would go back to the station and talk for 8 hours on-air. Sitting in that dark little studio by myself in the wee hours of the morning, well some nights it was a challenge just to stay awake.

But radio people are nothing if not creative!

I came up with a few ways to entertain myself. I'd turn up the tunes and do sit-ups on the floor. Sometimes I'd jump rope to the beat of whatever cd I was playing. I actually managed to perfect my skipping technique so I could jump without making the cd's skip.

I also loved propping all the studio doors open, cranking up the music, and then rollerblading around the empty news room and out into the parking lot. I bet you never imagined your favourite radio announcer doing stuff like that at work. Fortunately neither did my boss!

The truth is it can be pretty boring during those long lonely nights at the radio station, especially during long music sweeps. In fact I probably shouldn't admit this, but some nights I would bring in a good book and catch up on my reading.

One night it was me vs. a Charles Dickens classic. Charles won.

It was 4 in the morning and by page seven of "Great Expectations", I was ready for some quality naptime. And I had just the music for it. Guns N' Roses, Patience. It's a soothing mellow tune, close to 6 minutes long. Certainly enough time for a quick catnap.

I even had my own little alarm system. When the song had about 20 seconds left, the CD player would make a slight clicking noise. That little 'click' saved my butt on several napping occasions.

Except for this one.

I must have been really tired because I didn't hear a thing. I slept right through the warning "click". I slept through the final 20 seconds of the song. And then I slept through an hour of dead air.

I was groggily shaking my head when our newsgal burst into the control room screaming and almost tripping over me on the floor. "For heavens' sake! WAKE UP, ALI!!! PLAY SOMETHING!"

Announcers have definitely been fired for much less than that but I was lucky. To this day, my wonderful boss still laughs about it!

THE BEST PART

I love radio for so many reasons.

The main one? It's where I met my husband, Michael. We actually grew up 10 minutes from each other and my Mum was his grade five teacher. Years later we both went to Loyalist College for radio broadcasting (he was one year behind me).

We ended up working together, and we FINALLY hooked up and got married on Canada Day in 2005.

Years ago I produced a commercial with one line that I do truly believe: "Radio gets results!" In my case it's a gorgeous Canadian diamond and fantastic husband!

MICHELLE BODEN

630 CHED EDMONTON, ALBERTA
WWW.630CHED.COM

Michelle Boden began her news career in Vernon, BC in 1991. After a couple years in radio, Michelle decided to try television news at stations in both Terrace, BC and Lethbridge, Alberta. Then it was on to Edmonton, where Michelle became the news anchor at A-Channel.

Michelle has since returned to radio news and her current position at 630 CHED in Edmonton. She is producer and host of the documentary series, The Inside Story.

Michelle loves creating "theatre of the mind" through radio. She feels blessed to interview amazing people and introduce fascinating topics. Her documentary series, The Inside Story, has won The Solicitor General's Award, Regional and National RTNDA Awards for in-depth/investigative reporting, as well as the "Gold Ribbon Award" from the Canadian Association of Broadcasters (CAB).

MY BIG BREAK

I'll never forget my first job in radio, which was also when I covered my first Federal election. I was working the afternoon shift at a small station in Vernon, B.C. and I was assigned to interview Prime Minister Jean Chretien.

Someone with limited news experience rarely gets an opportunity to interview such a big name politician, but our senior reporter wasn't available. So it was passed on to me. The rookie!

I was going to interviewTHE PRIME MINISTER OF CANADA for Pete's sake! That's like a music lover interviewing the Rolling Stones. This could be myBIG BREAK! I ran back to my apartment in a flap to slip into something more professional,grab my gear and race to the news conference.

If you've ever seen a live news interview on tv, you'll notice reporters gather around the subject fighting to get the best interview position. We call that a media "scrum". Since this was the Prime Minister, the scrum was jam-packed with national media people.

It was the second time during the campaign that the PM stopped in small town BC, and the rumours were flying. Everyone was sure he had a HUGE announcement, affecting the future of all Canadians.

The National guys had all their top guns out to this news conference. I wastotally overwhelmed and under-experienced, surrounded by news people I'd only seen on TV. Well known reporters, big name producers, experienced audio and visual crews and VERY expensive equipment.

And then there was me. The rookie. Squished at the back of the scrum with my small town tape recorder. I felt like a plastic Fisher Price toy drowning in a sea of sleek Sony's.

But things took a strange turn.

I'm fluent in French. I knew that might win over our

distinguished Prime Minister, so I let a few French words slip out early in the media scrum. Chretien noticed and called me up to the front of the pack so he could hear my questions better. (Good thing because let's face it, he was a little hard to understand too.)

I charged right in asking the hard questions, bringing the news to my people. "The Rookie" as everyone thought of me, was on top of her game. I was on fire!

I should have known it was going too well.

At the end of the Q&A session, our honourable Prime Minister Jean Chretien leaned down to secretly say something to me. He singled me out in front of all of those national reporters, AND their tv crews.

OHMYGOSH! Was he going to give me a huge political scoop? Pass along hot news on a change in party policy? Whisper his secret recipe for French Vinaigrette? I leaned in close to Mr. Chretien, making sure thenetwork tv cameras had a great angle and crystal clear audio.

Visions of national news coverage danced in my head.

And then in front of the entire country, our Prime Minister spoke.

"Scuse me, Meee-chelle. I fear dat you are wearing de shoes of de separate colours. Dis one is black. Dat one is brown."

Nice.

Of course I made the blooper reels on that night's news broadcasts across Canada. I finally made it onto the national news!

ANDREA DUNN

FM96 LONDON, ONTARIO
WWW.FM96.COM

Andrea graduated from the Broadcasting program at Fanshawe College in 1999. Her first radio job was at Rock 95 in Barrie, Ontario, where Andrea worked for 5 years before moving back to London and a job at her favourite radio station, FM 96.

Andrea loves her job because it never feels like work. And her radio career has given her the opportunity to do some great things for the community. Andrea is most proud of her involvement with the London Abused Women's Centre and the local Aids Walk.

On a lighter note, Andrea's favourite on air moment was talking to Pearl Jam guitarist, Stone Gossard. She admits to being a huge fan of the band and says, "We had a great conversation that I'll archive forever!"

NICARAGUA

When I first began my radio career I never dreamed it would one day take me to Nicaragua and the experience of a lifetime.

During one of our regular staff meetings in October

of 2005, my boss mentioned that we might have an opportunity to team with World Vision in the coming months. I was incredibly excited at the thought. Travelling, charity work and radio – my three favourite things!

A few months later my boss sat me down and said that our World Vision campaign was going ahead and he would like me to go on the trip.

I think I cried. I was so honoured that I would get a chance to travel with a team from World Vision and see first hand the work that they're doing and the difference they make for children around the world.

We boarded a plane on route to Nicaragua, one of the most beautiful, yet poorest countries in the world. Looking out the window from the plane I remember thinking how lucky I was. I had no idea exactly what I was in for but I knew this trip would change my life.

It was January 18th, 2006, and a gorgeous sunny day when we landed in Managua, the capital of Nicaragua. Our World Vision team leader gave us an honest pep talk about the long week and the emotional moments ahead of us. Our group would be visiting sick children and their families in some of the most remote, poorest areas of the country.

The following morning we drove about an hour outside the capital city to a small place known as Quebrada Onda. This is where I met a young boy named David.

He lived with his mother and father, his brother and a number of other close relatives in a tiny shack the size of a single garage. The family was extremely poor and I found out that David was a very sick little kid, but his family couldn't afford medical treatment.

David had a simple medical condition, but because his family couldn't afford the treatment, his condition could be life threatening. I remember thinking, "that could never happen in our country. People would be outraged." I soon learned that it happened in Nicaragua every single day.

World Vision opened my eyes to what a global village we live in. And it reinforced how simple acts of kindness really go a long way to brighten the lives of others.

I came home with a new sense of hope and gratitude. And I realized again how lucky I am. My daily struggles in no way compare to David and his family.

I live in a beautiful, rich country. I have food and medical care. I get to go to work every day and hopefully make people smile.

This trip with World Vision has been both a career and a personal highlight.

LISA CAMERON

HOT 93 SASKATOON, SASKATCHEWAN
WWW.HOT93.COM

Lisa started her radio career in 1999. She's worked at stations in North Battleford, Grande Prairie, Medicine Hat and Lethbridge.

Lisa is now the afternoon drive host at Hot 93 in Saskatoon. She wakes up everyday thrilled to go to work and can't believe her job includes "duties" like interviewing country star Brad Paisley.

THE FRIDAY NIGHT POLKA PARTY

My very first radio job was in the friendly little town of North Battleford, Saskatchewan. I kicked off the weekends hosting a show called the "Friday Night Polka Party".

The radio station played all our music from cd, except for Friday nights. Our polka music was on record albums. I grew up listening to cassette tapes, so vinyl records were foreign objects to me.

Late one Friday Polka Night, I was relaxing with my feet up in the control room, and playing what felt like my millionth polka. That was the night I received THE CALL.

On the phone was a sweet elderly lady who had been listening to the show. She sounded very concerned, flustered and out of breath. "Hello Dear. I'm having a bit of a problem with your music tonight."

"I'm sorry," I apologized. "But it's Friday night. That means Polka night. But if it makes you feel better, I'm with you. I don't really like polka music either."

"No, no, no. I love the polkas," the sweet old woman said. "But I can't seem to dance."

WHAT???

Silence on my end. Then, "Gee, I'm sorry that you can't dance." That was my outside voice. My inside voice was saying, "You called me cause you can't dance? You've got to be kidding!" (Remember, I was 19 at the time.)

Then I hear her sweet little voice again. "Dear, I'm trying to polka and I just can't do it." Hmm. Okay.

My outside voice: "Well, I'm really sorry you can't dance. I'm not sure how I can help you with that. Maybe you could take some lessons or something."

My inside voice: "Good grief! Are you serious?"

"Oh dear," the elderly lady sighed. Now she's frustrated.

"You really don't understand. I can polka with the best of them. I was Miss Polka Saskatchewan in 1956. But tonight I can't keep up with the music. You're playing your records much much too fast, dear!"

Huh? Too fast?

I whipped my head around to stare down the turntable and for the first time I noticed there were three different speeds to run the albums. The needle was set on the highest speed. I was playing all the polkas in triple time. Not even the Chipmunks could have danced to that beat.

I had been sitting there listening to this polka music

all night long, and I hadn't even realized this. How many Fridays I had been playing all my polkas at triple speed?

I thought they were actually supposed to sound like that!

"CAN I MAKE A REQUEST?"

During our on air shift it feels like we get a zillion phone calls and a million different questions. I can't tell you how often I hear, "Can I request a song?"

Anotherpopular question we get usually starts like this. "I hope you can help me. I'm looking for the name of a song." I know this seems like a simple thing, after all we're SUPPOSED to be the experts.

Those callers never seem to know who the artist is. But they DO know the song has the word "love" in it somewhere.

And they remember FOR SURE we played it last Tuesday. Around noon. Or maybe it was Wednesday... Yes, it was definitely Wednesday. But it was at 3, not noon. Or maybe it was at 10:30.

When you're on the receiving end of this every day, it can get frustrating.

But I also know that listeners don't realize how busy we get in the control room. I think the perception is that we sit there with our feet up, listening tomusic, waiting for the phone to ring.

In reality, we're running contests, editing phone calls, planning weather and traffic breaks, trying to squeeze requests into regularly scheduled music and looking for a second to run to the bathroom. All in the minute or so before the song is over.

I remember one afternoon, an elderly man phoned

and asked for the name and artist of a song. The man spoke so softly I was straining to hear him, and finally told him to speak up. He knew the tune was by a male singer and as usual, the song had the word "love" in it.

I was in the middle of a contest and had about twenty-seven other things going on. I really did want to help him andwas sorting through my brain for the right tune but I had to keep putting him on hold. Quite honestly at the time I was thinking, "I don't care what this stupid song is! Don't you know how busy I am right now? Arrrrrrrrggghhh!"

I eventually figured outwhat he was looking for. It was a sweet love song by Collin Raye, called "Love Me".

I remember blurting out the title and singer, so relieved I could hang up the phone and get back to my 'real' work.

Although I was quite abrupt, the elderly man was gracious. "Thank you very much", he said quietly. "My wife just died and I wanted to play this at her funeral. She really loved this song. She made me dance to it all the time."

In about two seconds I went from feeling rushed and curt, to totally embarrassed. Suddenly I felt tears in my eyes. I was really ashamed at myself for getting frustrated with this polite elderly man who just lost his wife.

All he wanted was help with a song. Her favorite song. To play at her funeral.

I will never forget that phone call. It's those memories that make me love my job more and more everyday. And realize how lucky I am.

MELISSA WRIGHT

K-ROCK 97.3 EDMONTON, ALBERTA
WWW.K-ROCK973.COM

Melissa began her radio career covering community events foran Edmonton station when she was 21. She left for a job at Chyme FM in Kitchener, but has returned to her hometown of Edmonton and has been at K-Rock for the past ten years.

Melissa loves her job: the hours are perfect, and she's surrounded by fun, creative people. Plus, she's had the opportunity to meet and interview some of her favourite rock stars; from Sammy Hagar and David Lee Roth, to Deep Purple and Supertramp.

If Melissa were not in radio, she'd love to work with an animal charity. Melissa is a member of the WWE; she works with the Edmonton Humane Society, and is also a big supporter of PETA. Melissa has her own family of animals at home; Sadie, the cat, and a pug named Nubbin, which she received from a listener.

"EXTRA LARGE DOUBLE DOUBLE, PLEASE..."

What do you think is the hardest thing about being a radio announcer? Working overnights and holidays? The expectation to be upbeat on-air, even when you're having a rotten day? Getting a paycheque most people laugh at?

Surprisingly it's none of the above. The most challenging part of being on the air is trying to carefully eat your lunch at work without spilling anything on the soundboard.

Talk about pressure! The soundboard in the on air studio is our temple. We sit in front of our soundboard like you sit at your desk at work. Except, the top of our desk is an intricate mass of buttons, wires and sliding volume controls. Everything you hear coming out of your speaker is controlled from the soundboard, including songs, commercials and our microphones.

And every announcer knows the golden rule of radio. DO NOT SPILL ANYTHING ON THE SOUNDBOARD! Keep any sort of wet substance far, far away. Any little spill, even a couple drips of coffee could result in frying the wires and killing the station.

That's where my story starts.

I am Canadian, which means my morning commute to work includes a stop at Tim Hortons for my daily extra large double double.

You see where this is going, don't you?

I had set my extra large double double on the counter next to the soundboard. Turning around to flip a switch, I knocked my very wet, very full cup of coffee across the entire board. I re-live that traumatic moment in my head every day. Sometimes twice a day. Always in slow motion.

Picture it. One minute there's music blaring in the control room, the next second there's a hissing, crackling, zap, zap, zap. ZAP. Then NOTHING. Dead air. The board was cooked.

It's not like I shoot super soakers around the control

room. Or juggle water balloons over the soundboard. All I did was spill my coffee. It was a workplace accident.

But as a listener, all YOU know for sure is that there's nothing coming out of your speakers. Nada. Zero. Zilch. Silence.

Announcers have been fired for less.

Red faced and panicky, I called our engineer Doug to the control room and quickly explained what happened. Like a superhero he sprung into action: he kicked one of our producers out of his studio, re-routed some cables and had me back on the air in a matter of minutes.

I was still freaked out. After all, I had just single-handedly destroyed the audio board AND taken out the station. I vowed never to bring a coffee into the control room again.

Which is why when Doug came into the makeshift control room to ask me if I took cream and sugar in my coffee, I responded, "Shouldn't you worry about fixing this mess, before you get me another coffee???"

He stared at me for a second, and then left the room shaking his head. That's when it hit me. Coffee loaded with cream and sugar would be harder on the wires and control panel then plain black coffee.

Doug was actually trying to figure out how much damage was done. He wasn't offering to get me another coffee!

DEE
(DIANE JAROWAY)

ROCK 94 THUNDER BAY, ONTARIO
WWW.ROCK94.COM

Diane Jaroway (Dee) says her on-air passion began back in grade two. When all the other kids were playing dodge ball during recess, Dee would wander the schoolyard with her Barbie tape recorder looking for breaking news and playground scandals.

After graduatingfrom Television Broadcasting at Confederation College in 2001,Dee has enjoyed several cool jobs in media including: production assistant, studio camera operator, reporter, editor and master control.

Dee is currently the morning show co-host at Rock 94 in Thunder Bay. She loves her job and everyone she works with, but admits she'd leave it all in a heartbeat for a happy ending with Johnny Depp!

SAVE THE BLING!!

One of my favourite things about being a radio announcer is interviewing musicians live on air. Of course, when a band is in town it's usually to perform a concert.

Which leads me to the scariest thing about being a radio announcer... standing up in front of a rowdy crowd of music lovers and emceeing a live show.

Imagine yourself, all alone on a huge stage with a blinding spotlight shining directly on YOU. A hush falls over the crowd and everyone stares at you, waiting. Toss in the pressure of having to remember the name of your radio station, the venue, and the band. If you're really nervous it's hard to remember your own name, never mind all the other stuff.

The first time I had to emcee a concert, I was mortified. I didn't have regular butterflies in my tummy; I had the butterflies on speed. They were bouncing around in there like they just drank 8 pots of coffee.

A little nervous energy is a good thing but this was ridiculous.

I stumbled onto the stage ready to blank out. Or pass out. Whichever came first. I opened my mouth to greet the audience and a strange thing happened. The butterflies disappeared. I introduced myself, joked around a bit and really got the crowd going.

The band was waiting in the wings and the concert hall was electric with excitement. The music started and of course the crowd went wild. With every passing second onstage I gained more confidence. I raised my voice to scream the name of the band and fling my arms out to welcome them to our awesome city.

And in slow motion I saw my bling go flying off my wrist. About 20 pounds of jewellery, sailing through the air in the direction of the band. (Okay it was only one little gold bracelet, but at that moment it felt like huge rap star bling.)

I was mortified. Did everyone see that? Did I hit someone in the band? Where the heck is my bracelet? What should I do? Leave the bracelet on stage for the band to stomp on? NO WAY. I am woman, hear me roar!

The stage was a mass of coloured lights as the band launched into their first number. My job onstage was over but I didn't care.

I dropped to my hands and knees and started crawling around in search of my poor defenceless bracelet. I spotted something shiny on the floor at the front of the stage and crawled over. Darn it! Just a speaker connector.

I slowly crawled past the lead singer as they began their second number. Hopefully no one trips over me. Somewhere in the back of my mind it registered how dirty the floor was, but I didn't care. My beautiful little bracelet was lying scared and alone somewhere on this huge stage.

I tried to shield my eyes from the glaring spotlight and saw a glint of gold under the drum kit. I quickly crawled past the drummer and leaned over as far I could under his drums. Yes! There it was. My bracelet had landed directly under the snare drum. I inched in a little further, careful not to knock over the cymbals. I accidentally touched the drummer's leg. He kicked out at me. Oops! One more grab and ... GOT IT! MY BRACELET WAS SAFE! WHEW!

Relieved, I looked up to see the drummer staring down at me with a dirty look.

"Get away from my feet!!" Oops, right. They're trying to do a concert up here! I tenderly cradled my bracelet and half standing, half crouching I frog-hopped off the stage.

I explained what happened on-air the next morning, but I never did get a chance to tell the guys in the band. I can imagine the stories floating around on the tour circuit. "Remember that girl in Thunder Bay who introduced us, then crawled around the stage, and felt up the drummer's leg?'

JACKIE RAE GREENING

CFCW EDMONTON, ALBERTA
WWW.CFCW.COM

Jackie Rae is an award winning radio announcer at CFCW in Edmonton, Alberta. She was awarded the Canadian Country Music Association's 'On-Air Personality of the Year', Major market, for 2004 and 2005.

Jackie Rae started her radio career in 1982 at CKGY in Red Deer. After on-air gigs in Westlock, Drumheller, and CHQT Edmonton, Jackie Rae was hired at CFCW in 1989.

She still loves the variety of her job and the wonderful way radio can touch people. Her co-host of many years Wes Montgomery, passed away in April of 2005, and Jackie admits it was CFCW listeners that carried the show for the rest of the week, not her. Their heartfelt response was amazing. Just like family.

NAME THAT TUNE

I've been in country radio since 1982 and I absolutely love it. Especially when I can sneak out of the studio and hang out with our listeners at station events.

I've hosted just about everything. Concerts, community events, charity functions and talent shows. I've stood outside freezing during a May snowstorm at a 4-H Cattle Show. I've alsohosted the opening ceremonies at the Canadian Men's Curling Championship.

But the gig that stands out most in my mind was emceeing the finals of the Youth Talent Search during Klondike Days in Edmonton.

The young performers hit the stage quickly, one after another, showing off their musical talents in search of the grand prize. As the emcee I had to introduce each act and keep the show running on time.

That's where my story begins.

The sound tech and I had devised a system to keep things rolling. During my moments on-stage, the tech would flash a green light when the next kid was ready to go. If he flashed a red light, the upcoming performer was NOT ready and I had to keep talking and kill time on stage.

Following one particular novelty act, I was stranded on stage for what felt like forever. I don't know what the glitch was, but the tech kept flashing me the red light, which meant I had to kill time.

I'm pretty good at ad-libbing, but I was running out of things to say and it was getting a little uncomfortable. For both the audience and myself.

That's when I glanced down and noticed the last performer left his recorder on stage. Remember those brown flutes we were forced to play in elementary school? I was relieved to have a gimmick to help me kill some time, so I started a little game of 'Name That Tune' with the audience.

Apparently my flute skills are lacking because the crowd thought this was hilarious. Every time I blew into that recorder, the audience burst out laughing.

Gosh, I thought. I must be really bad!

The more I tried to play, the harder everyone laughed. Some of the folks even covered their faces with their hands so they didn't have to see me play. I could actually hear them groaning.

I had no idea I was so tone-deaf. This was really embarrassing.

Suddenly, the voice of an angel was whispering softly in my ear. Actually it was my sound tech murmuring in my earpiece. He must be ready to go. Thank goodness.

I struggled to hear the tech's muffled words in my left ear. "Blah, blah, blah, ...the snowboarder with his toes". Huh?

It was really hard to hear him above the crowd who was still laughing at my attempts to play the recorder. I could tell the audience was feeling my pain. They almost looked embarrassed for me.

I adjusted my earpiece in time to catch more murmuring from my tech. It was so muffled. What the heck was he saying?

"Blah, blah, blah... laying the flea border with his hose!" WHAAAT??? Was my audio tech drunk?

There I was standing in the middle of the stage at Klondike Days, surrounded by thousands of giggling music fans. I had a stunned smile pasted on my face and some kids' recorder hanging limply from my lips. And in my earpiece the sound tech was murmuring,"playing the recorder with his nose".

I had just played 5 rounds of Name That Tune with the audience. The recorder hanging out of my mouth was left behind by a kid...who had been playing it WITH HIS NOSE.

LAURIE HEALY

CHANNEL 4 FM
DUBAI, UNITED ARAB EMIRATES

Laurie Healy has always envied those with undeniable talent: musicians, athletes, artists, people that can build things. She decided that with no natural ability to garner an Olympic medal or even a Juno Award, she'd attempt what seemed like the best job in the world: a radio dj.

Laurie remembers listening to the radio every morning on the hour-long bus ride from the farm up to her school in Vulcan (a little town in southern Alberta...joke amongst yourselves!)

Laurie loved the effect radio had on her – the power it had to make her laugh, cry or feel pride. She wanted to get in on the magic, so she pursued a radio career and has worked at stations in Medicine Hat, Red Deer, Edmonton, Calgary, and most recently, Dubai in the United Arab Emirates.

THE HEART OF THE NIGHT

At one point in my radio career I was host of the evening show at EZ Rock in Edmonton. "Heart of the Night" was a relationship show that combined relaxing music and lots of on-air calls.

Listeners were encouraged to share stories and give us a glimpse into their lives.

I learned a lot about people during that show. And I learned from everyone. Singles and couples, straight and gay, young and old.

We got calls from passionate couples madly in love or having a fight. Teens ecstatic about their first romance, and middle-aged listeners sharing the pain of divorce.

I heard from lovers celebrating milestone anniversaries, and one couple actually called me from their bedroom. Guess what they were doing? (Thank goodness we taped the calls instead of airing them live!)

The most heartbreaking moment happened one night when I spoke to a young woman who admitted her husband was physically abusing her.

She was listening to the show and she needed someone to talk to. Her story was so sad and so real. She was suffering terrible physical and mental abuse at the hands of someone she loved. It was a dangerous situation, and every woman's worst nightmare.

Between silence and tears, she shared an incredibly private and emotional story of being physically beaten by someone she trusted. I scrambled to find the phone numbers of local support agencies.

And I asked her if I could air part of her call on the radio. It was so heartfelt and I knew it could provide strength to other women listening.

The young woman was silent for a minute, thinking about my request. But suddenly she nervously said "no", and hung up.

I understood. It takes a lot of courage to share your private hell.

Minutes later the same young woman called back. She changed her mind. She wanted me to air her story and maybe help other women by sharing her terrible experience with abuse.

She only asked to remain anonymous.

I never heard from her again. But after I aired her chilling story, so many other listeners phoned in with words of genuine concern and support for her. I also took calls from women who understood all too well what she was going through.

It was a raw and difficult show. Both heartbreaking and encouraging.

That happened years ago, but I still think about that young woman sometimes. I hope with all my heart that she got out of that relationship and created a wonderful life for herself.

Speaking of life, a few weeks later I received another emotional call during the show, this time from a couple in the delivery room! They had brought a radio to the hospital and were listening while mom-to-be was in labour.

The husband was so excited he could barely talk. He even put his wife on the phone for a second. She sounded exhausted! No kidding – SHE'S IN LABOUR! I'm positive she was about to hurl the phone back at her husband any second. That's what I would have done.

I can't remember if they had a boy or girl. I do remember thinking that people call the radio station at the oddest times!

LEANNE CATER

COUNTRY 95.3 TORONTO, ONTARIO
WWW.COUNTRY953.COM

Leanne Cater is a country radio veteran and a huge Ottawa Senators fan.

She also admits to being a dedicated follower of the Church of Mixology. When not exploring new recipes with friends, Lea can be found browsing in her favourite store, the LCBO (Liquor Control Board of Ontario).

Lea is also an animal lover, and doesn't mind being upstaged regularly by her cat "Joshua Joseph (The Technicolor Dreamcat)", or her Dwarf Lion's Head rabbit, "Edward VonRockstar the 3rd". Lea encourages everyone to find pet-love at there local Humane Society.

WHACKING THE GLASS CEILING

As women on any career path know, that "glass ceiling" can be very real.

Co-workers who started in your industry at the same level as you (or maybe began their career after you did) keep getting the choice jobs. Their stars keep rising while yours seems inexplicably tethered.

Then you notice a common thread among these people. None of them wear bras (that you know of!) They're men. Sound familiar?

The broadcasting industry is definitely not an exception to this unwritten rule. Although it has changed considerably over the years, it wasn't that long ago that I was told I 'need not apply' for a particular position, because I wasn't a man.

No question, I was frustrated. But instead of raising a stink I decided to raise eyebrows, thinking perhaps a little humour would get my point across more effectively.

The day after receiving the news that I "didn't have what it took" to apply for the job, I cycled to work.

Upon arrival I headed for the make-shift ping pong table set up in the lounge area of the radio station, snagged a couple of the ping pong balls and made a bee-line for the boss's office.

Just before I reached his door, I slipped the ping-pong balls up the leg of my spandex bike shorts and strategically 'placed' them. Then I leaned up against the doorframe and told him that I'd like to apply for the job, as I believed I finally had what they were looking for.

He looked up at me in puzzlement and I glanced downward at my ping-pong balls. He followed my gaze, and got an eyeful of what I was eluding to.

"What the-- ...LEANNE! That's (expletive) disgusting!"

"Yup", I said. "That's pretty much how I feel about the whole situation too!" With that, I turned and walked away.

It didn't make any difference with the job that time around but I certainly felt better!

For the record, the guy they DID hire for that position didn't last. I eventually landed the job and held it for close to 6 years. (Victory is mine! MmmWAHAHAHAA.. eh hem...)

I have since made the jump to a morning show in Toronto, and I absolutely love it. Radio is an awesome business. It's fun and challenging and if you can keep your sense of humour and your nose to the grindstone, it can be very rewarding.

EILEEN BELL

630 CHED EDMONTON, ALBERTA
WWW.630CHED.COM

Eileen began her broadcast career in Provo, Utah, at KBYU-TV & FM in 1979. In February of 1982 she moved to Red Deer, Alberta and morning news on CFCR-FM, Canada's only fm country music station at the time. Eileen was soon promoted to News Director for both CFCR and CKRD AM.

In April of '84, Eileen landed a job at 630 CHED in Edmonton, and she has called CHED home for the past 20+ years.

Eileen is currently one of the hosts of the "630 CHED Afternoon News" magazine program. She loves the constantly changing subject matter, and the opportunity to interview pretty well anyone she likes.

According to Eileen: "I love the 'make it or break it" feeling in radio. It's you and your brains on the line during a live interview, and your sense of humour can shine or fall flat. And of course it's a rush to have Ken Dryden or Donny Osmond return my calls!"

START SPREADIN' THE NEWS

In December of 2003 I found out that I have Type 2 Diabetes.

This health news followed years and years of free food that restaurants sent to the radio station. In fact my weight had almost doubled in the 20 years I worked at CHED. (If I gave you more specific numbers – I'd have to kill you!)

The diabetes was a huge wake-up call for me and I got to work reducing my weight. My battle with diabetes, including diet and exercise, was closely chronicled on the air since thousands of Canadians face the same diagnosis each month. As the pounds fell away my health radically improved, and one year later I was 100 pounds lighter.

On September 1, 2005 I was broadcasting live from the Alberta Legislature grounds as CHED carried provincial Centennial celebrations.

Before the broadcast began I had a chance to meet several loyal CHED listeners, one in particular who had been following my weight loss progress. Quite closely.

The stranger introduced himself and said he admired my courage in my battle with diabetes. He was speaking very loud and I could tell he was a little hard of hearing.

I was extremely flattered when he said I was an inspiration, but then the conversation jumped into uncomfortable territory.

This same man, who I had known for all of 90 seconds, suddenly eyed me up and down and asked (yelled) if I was planning on losing more weight.

I hesitated and then said, "Yes. Another fifty pounds would be great."

"HUH?" he grunted. Oh right, he was hard of hearing.

I raised my voice. "I SAID I WANT TO LOSE ANOTHER FIFTY POUNDS!" A few glances came our way, but nothing I couldn't handle.

After a few more minutes of circular and uncomfortably loud conversation with this same gentleman, I explained I had to go on air soon. I really did appreciate his concern, but I had to get my thoughts together for the live broadcast.

We said genial goodbyes and I went back to work. But the dear soul apparently wasn't finished with me. He decided that more people should hear my story.

The Alberta Legislature grounds were packed with Centennial Day revellers, and as my new friend wandered away he stopped almost everyone he encountered. I could actually see him pointing back at me and basically yelling out my story.

After the first 10 or 20 folks, he condensed it down to one sentence. "THAT'S EILEEN BELL FROM CHED – SHE'S GOT TO LOSE ABOUT FIFTY POUNDS!"

Then they would both look at me. Of course I would blush. And my new friend would happily continue on his way, spreading my health news to half of Edmonton.

And no doubt meaning very well.

SANDRA PLAGAKIS

105.3 KISS FM OTTAWA, ONTARIO
WWW.1053KISSFM.COM

Sandra graduated from the broadcasting program at Algonquin College in 1993. Her first gig straight out of college was weekend news anchor and reporter at a station in Brockville, Ontario.

Soon Sandra was off to Toronto and her big break at 102.1 The Edge. She was the afternoon news anchor and eventually moved up to the morning show, where she worked with some of the best radio teams in the country.

Sandra is currently the morning show co-host on 105.3 Kiss FM with her pals Carter and The Boyle. After 13 years she loves her job and still gets a huge kick out of radio.

ME AND MY BRIAN

I have gone on record many times admitting my love for figure skating. How many on-air debates have I had about the merits of figure skating as a sport? Too many to mention.

Like many Canadians I was glued to the TV during the '88 Calgary Olympics, watching "the Battle of the Brians".

And years later I finally had the opportunity to meet one of my all time heroes, Brian Orser. It was at a fundraising event in Ottawa, where Brian was offering up an item for the silent auction; a private skate *with him* on the Rideau Canal. *Hell - oooo!*

Of course I bid on it. Then I cornered him.

Without taking a single breath, I gushed for five minutes about how great he was and how I was dying to skate with him. I think I even commented on how little he was (because that's what every man wants to hear).

I've never seen such a wide-eyed look of fear, as I did in his eyes that day. I actually remember thinking "I'm freaking him out", but not really caring because I was talking to THE Brian Orser.

I was called away for a second. And strangely enough, when I turned around he was long gone.

To add insult to injury I didn't win the silent auction either. In fact I'm pretty sure I saw HIM writing in a fake name that was eventually the winning bid.

Oh well. I still love figure skating.

SEX IN A TENT

Have you ever seen a couple have sex in a tent? Have you ever seen a couple have sex in a tent, 10 feet away from you? Have you ever seen a couple have sex in a tent, 10 feet away from you while you were working?

Years ago when I worked in Toronto, we were having one of those crazy contests where we asked our listeners to perform insane stunts. You couldn't qualify for the grand prize unless you performed an idiotic stunt.

One task was to have sex in a tent.

We had actually set up a tent in-studio, dimmed the lights, and put a light inside so we were able to see silhouettes and confirm the act was being completed.

A newly married couple volunteered. They showed up at our studio at 7 in the morning to do the deed.

And you can't pull off a stunt like this without an audience. Someone actually came by with a lawn chair to watch. True story! (We were all just waiting for him to whip out his popcorn and 3D glasses!)

Without going into detail, I remember being totally mesmerized by the effort these two put into the contest. It was like a car wreck. I could not turn away.

The couple finished with an excellent dismount. Too bad it wasn't a skating event. The Russian judge would have given them a 6.

They left the studio with a smile on their faces. And no, they didn't win the grand prize...but some might argue they weren't losers either.

Some days I just have to shake my head and laugh at some of the things I do at "work".

KACEY WILSON

CJOB 68 WINNIPEG, MANITOBA
WWW.CJOB.COM

Kacey Wilson began her radio career in 2000 as a reporter in small town, BC. After a quick stop in Prince George, Kacey moved to Winnipeg where she is host/producer of the drive home current affairs show, "Today So Far" on CJOB 68.

Kacey loves many things about her job. How radio allows you to tell a story; being able to report events as they are unfolding; delivering that message to thousands of listeners.

And undeniably, the best part of Kacey's job is the fascinating people she's met along the way.

EVERYDAY HEROES

I work at a news/talk station, which means a huge part of my job is doing interviews. And here's a secret I've never shared with anyone. It's not the celebrities or the politicians that have made the most impact on me. It's our everyday heroes; the community leaders dedicated to making their hometown a better place to live; or those people who have faced adversity and become someone they've always dreamed of being.

I've interviewed politicians, entertainers, criminals, parents, athletes, teenagers, protesters and many police officers. News happens so fast, and sometimes the day is such a blur that I forget most of those conversations by the next newscast.

But one interview in particular had such a profound impact I still think about it today. It goes back a few years ago to a lovely autumn afternoon. I had invited three local women into the studio to promote an upcoming fundraiser for breast cancer research. But the day turned into so much more. These women were incredibly special.

All three ladies had fought and survived breast cancer.

My plan was to put a face to the disease that affects so many people, and these women were all very well spoken.

They shared personal, painful, private stories. And 'highly emotional' doesn't even begin to describe this interview.

The three survivors had all struggled with their changing bodies. The balding heads. The horrific nausea from chemotherapy. And of course, losing a part of their bodies that defined their femininity.

They talked openly about death. Their biggest fear wasn't dying. It was dying before they had a chance to see their children grow up.

I was in total awe of these women and their bravery. There were moments during the interview when all four of us were in tears. I had to cut to commercials several times to compose myself.

But amid the sadness and the tragedy in their stories, there was so much hope. The three survivors spoke about how conquering breast cancer had changed their entire lives, and how they looked at the world. They now took the time to really enjoy and appreciate the small things.

I wasn't the only one so profoundly impacted by these women. Many other listeners phoned the station in tears, to share their own stories. And to thank these women for their courage.

That interview has never left me. I think of those three survivors often. Especially when I need to be reminded how precious life really is.

I love my job.

LAURA ZAINA

MAGIC 99.9 THUNDER BAY, ONTARIO
WWW.MAGIC999.FM

Laura Zaina is the morning show co-host and newsgal at Magic 99.9 in Thunder Bay. Like every other career gal, Laura has held a lot of different positions before being offered her dream job. She was a production assistant at a television station. She was a tv weather anchor, and a commercial director. Laura also worked at a hospital for a couple of years as a dietary assistant, where she loved her coworkers but quickly realized 'radio' was where she really wanted to be.

In 2002, Laura accepted a position as morning show co-host and newsgal at Magic 99.9 in Thunder Bay, and she's never looked back.

MOMS EVERYWHERE, I SALUTE YOU!

I am a busy mom. I have three kids, a hubby, and a million responsibilities at home. Oh, and a few jobs. This isn't so unlike many other parents out there, and I think sometimes we sit back and wonder exactly how we managed to get everything done!

I started my radio career in 2001 as a news co-host, and I'm proud to have worked at several different stations in my hometown of Thunder Bay.

Radio is fun, exciting and fast paced. Every day is different, the people are wacky and quirky. I've made some friends for life. But I'll be honest – when you start out, the money is not that great. I've usually had to work several jobs at once to support my radio 'habit'. At one point I was doing the morning news on-air, and I also had a part time job in the dietary office at a hospital. I was a radio newswoman from 4:30am until 9am, and then it was off to the hospital until 2pm, then back home to be a wife and mom until bedtime. (This crazy shift called for an 8pm bedtime. I was usually sleeping *before* my youngest child!)

I obviously love radio AND the people I work with because I'm still doing it. And thankfully, the money gets much better after a few years.

In the meantime, I've managed to develop some incredible organizational skills, juggling my jobs, my home life, my hubby and my three kids. I actually think being a mom has really helped my career.

No matter what happens at work, it's really never that bad.

After all, I've been in labour three times.

I KNOW real pain.

MELANIE RISDON

96.9 JACK FM CALGARY, ALBERTA
WWW.JACKFM.CA

Melanie Risdon was born and raised in Calgary. As a Broadcast graduate ofMount Royal College, she was hired by news/talk station QR77 to drive the community cruiser to events through out Calgary. Mel quickly moved to full time traffic reporting on both QR and Power 107 where she stayed for 5 years.

Melanie left Calgary for a position at Hot 103 FM in Victoria, but missing friends and family she returned to her hometown within a year, and took a job at CJAY 92.

In 2004 Mel found her real radio home at JACK FM. Mel is thrilled to be back in her hometown where she lives happily ever after with her hubby, James and son, T.J.

"THE STAMPS HAVE WON THE CUP!"

I've had many embarrassing moments in my radio career, but there is one that seems to stick with me. I'd love to forget it but listeners constantly remind me of it even years later.

At the time of the 'incident' I was working for Power 107 and QR77. We often hosted "Power Parties", or live on location broadcasts from different Calgary bars.

On that fateful night I was hosting a Power Party at Outlaws. It was Retro night and the place was jam packed with retro lovers dressed in all their Austin Power's inspired outfits. Shagadelic, baby.

It was a few days after the Calgary Stampeders had won the Grey Cup, and when I arrived at the club I found out a bunch of the Stamps would be joining us with the actual Grey Cup.

Holy cow! I was a huge Stamps fan, actually a big CFL fan. I don't wanna brag but I know a thing or two about football.

We were all waiting for the Stamps and the Grey Cup to appear. In the meantime I had pre-recorded my cut-in, just to make sure the station had something ready to air.

Suddenly I heard loud cheers and screams at the entrance to the bar. The huge crowd started chanting "Go, Stamps, GO" and seconds later members of the Stamps were boisterously parading into the bar hoisting that beautiful Grey Cup above their heads. I could almost smell the testosterone.

I'm a radio pro and it's all about capturing the 'moment'. I COULD NOT let this go by without getting the excitement on-air. In a rush I called back to the station. "The Stamps are here with the Cup!" I yelled. "Dump my last cut-in. Throw me on live!"

And they did. Talk about exciting. "The Calgary Stampeders are with us at Outlaws right now, celebrating their recent victory." My voice was almost drowned out by the screaming and cheering in the background so I cranked up the volume.

"COME ON DOWN AND MEET OUR CFL CHAMPS AND SEE THE STANLEY CUP!" I yelled. "JOIN US AND SIP CHAMPAGNE FROM THE ACTUAL STANLEY

CUP!"

I screamed on for a solid minute about how "the Stamps were hoisting the STANLEY CUP, fans could get their picture taken with the STANLEY CUP. I got to hold the STANLEY CUP. The STANLEY CUP is huge!" Blah, blah, blah.

I was a little out of breath but I managed to give a full 60 second report about how the Calgary Stampeders won the Stanley Cup. Nobody stopped me and nobody corrected me. I was so caught up in the moment I didn't realize my mistake.

Minutes later this young guy walked up to me with a huge smirk on his face. He had just pulled into the parking lot and heard my live cut-in. And he got to the point quickly. It was *NOT* the Stanley Cup, dummy. That's hockey.

The Stamps had won the Grey Cup.

To top off the embarrassment, I actually worked at QR77. The "Official Voice of the Calgary Stampeders".

RACE

HOT 89.9 FM OTTAWA, ONTARIO
WWW.HOT899.COM

Race started her radio career in 2001 at The Team 1090 in Kitchener, Ontario. She's also worked at Majic 100 and is now at The New Hot 89.9 in Ottawa.

Race loves everything about her job: the hours, her listeners and the dynamic people she works with every day. But she says if radio doesn't work out, she'll attempt her back up career choice. Trophy wife.

PLUSHHHH SHHHHERTA SHHHHEEEEP

I've always wanted braces. Ever since I was a kid, I've had a crowded mouth full of teeth. By the time I hit my early 20's I was ready for braces. Unfortunately I was in college at the time, and could barely afford Kraft dinner and beer, never mind braces.

Last year one of my co-workers introduced me to her dentist, who noticed I always smiled with my mouth closed. I shared my crooked teeth insecurities with him. He in turn offered me a great deal on braces.

Are you kidding me? I jumped at the chance. I was a little wary that they would affect my speech, but the thought of straight teeth almost had me drooling. I decided to go for it.

My new dentist assured me that the brackets, which would be placed on the outside of my teeth, would not be intrusive. My boss was sceptical, but I was ecstatic.

The night before my dentist appointment I was so excited I couldn't sleep. It was Brace-mas Eve and I was in a constant fog, daydreaming about my new million dollar smile.

My dreams came to a crashing halt the following day when I slid into the dentist chair. Out of nowhere my new dentist pulls out this huge metal contraption that fits in the top of your mouth to expand your bite.

My dentist called it an appliance. Some people call it a spacer. I call it 'WAY TOO BIG TO FIT IN MY MOUTH'!

"You need it," my dentist assured me. "We can't straighten your teeth without it."

Whooooa! Nobody mentioned putting a tire jack in my mouth. I knew this contraption would mess with my speech, but I was already in the chair. I was guaranteed that this 'appliance' wouldn't obstruct my tongue too much, so I squeezed out all the bad vibes and gave them the go ahead. Bring on the tire jack!

My co-workers were eager to see me with my new braces, so I swung by the station after my appointment so they could examine me.

As soon as I walked in my boss called me into his office. "Talk," he commanded. "I want to hear what it sounds like!"

The second I started to speak a big hunk of spit flew out of my mouth! I can laugh now, but at the time I was pretty scared I'd be pulled off the air. Or even canned.

I had actually booked the week off work since I

figured I'd need some time alone with my new braces. My boss sent me on my way hoping I'd get used to them.

I did. Sort of. The hunk of metal wire didn't affect my on air performance, but I had a tough time recording commercials because of the silence in the recording studio. The microphone picked up every pop, hiss and slurp I made.

The most humiliating thing happened when I was asked to voice a commercial for Sleep Country Canada. I had to say that they were giving away Plush Serta Sheep.

I don't know about you, but most people *without* braces have a hard time saying that. Plush Serta Sheep. Plush Serta Sheep.

Now imagine saying it with braces. "Plushhhsh SShhhherta SShhhheep!" Ack. I did about a hundred takes as the producer laughed his head off, and then finally told me he'd ask someone else to voice the spot. I have a feeling that was his plan all along. He just wanted to torture me for a while.

I have since gotten the braces removed and I must say, they were worth it. I LOVE my teeth.

But I'll never forget how much effort it took to say "Plushhhsh SShhhherta SShhhheep". Effort and a lot of Kleenex.

CRYSTAL LILLY

97.5 THE RIVER KAMLOOPS, BC
WWW.CKRV.COM

Crystal grew up in the tiny town of 100 Mile House, BC. She got a taste of media in high school while writing for the local newspaper, 'The Free Press'. After graduation she went to school at UCC in Kamloops.

In 2004, Crystal received her Broadcasting diploma from BCIT in Vancouver. She worked as a reporter at Shaw TV in Kamloops for almost a year, but was quickly scooped up by sister stations 97.5 The River and CHNL AM Radio.

To this day Crystal's mom still reminds her that 'it took her awhile to start talking, but once she did she just never quit'!

BEWARE THE OPEN MICROPHONE

One of the first rules you learn in broadcasting is: *BEWARE THE OPEN MICROPHONE.* Microphones are sneaky little monsters. Whether you're in radio or tv, microphones can be a career killer.

The trick is to pretend they're always on. That way you never say anything stupid, rude or dumb that accidentally goes to air.

Somehow this rule escaped me the first time I did a live on-location for TV.

I was extremely nervous but it was actually a pretty simple task. I had to introduce a story live on camera, then throw it to some pre-taped footage. At the end I would come back on live to wrap it up. Simple.

The intro went off without a hitch. And I'm sure my relief was apparent to everyone. Live tv is really nerve-wracking for a rookie.

At the end of the story, my camera operator cued me up and gave me the mic. I went over my lines under my breath and seconds before going on-air I did a final check on my appearance.

"Hey, do I have any boogers on my face?" I asked the camera guy. Silence.

And in that split second I saw the look on his face and realized we were live. He started laughing, at first to himself, then out loud and finally he was shaking so hard he almost dropped his camera.

And I just stood there. Stunned.

Why I chose that particular phrase still baffles me. I've never said the word 'booger' in my life. But of course, the first time I use it the entire tv watching population of Kamloops hears it.

"Do I have any boogers on my face?"

Moral of my story: Unless you wanna be known as 'Booger Girl' for the rest of your career, BE WARY OF LIVE MICROPHONES!

LEXINE STEPHENS

Q107 FM CALGARY, ALBERTA
WWW.Q107FM.CA

Lexine is originally from Orangeville, Ontario. Her radio career has taken her across Canada from London to Toronto, Sarnia, Kelowna, Victoria and now Calgary where Lex is host of the drive home show at Q107 FM.

Lex loves the outdoors: hiking, skiing, skating and swimming. And her two best friends in the world are her sweetheart, Jason, and her bunny, Manhattan.

MY OOPS

There comes a time in everyone's radio career when there's a BIG "oops" moment. Live on air. Mine was HUGE and pretty vulgar.

1998 I was working in Kelowna at 99.9FM, the Bullet. Our music was on hard drive and we used a computer touch screen to play it on-air. I was hosting a live request show at the time, having a great day when suddenly my computer screen froze.

And out of my mouth came the most horrible words. I must have screamed curses for 2 minutes straight. I didn't even realize I KNEW so many bad words.

Not very professional. But at least my microphone wasn't on. In most on air studios there's a red button that lights up when your microphone is live. That's the only way we know we're on the air.

The control room door was closed, but one of the office gals had been walking by the studio window. As soon as I started cussing at the frozen computer her head whipped around like she'd been slapped.

I still remember the look of shock and horror on her face. And I read her lips through the studio window.

"LEX! YOUR MIC IS ON!" She motioned frantically to the microphone.

I look down at my red microphone light. Lying there quietly. Minding it's own business. Clearly off. "NO, IT'S NOT." I yell at her through the window.

"YES, IT IS!"

"NO, IT'S NOT!!!" I scream back at her.

"YES, IT IS!" I see her wildly bobbing her head up and down! "IT'S ON!" Within seconds the control room was full of people including our station engineer. He fiddled with the audio board and finally figured out that when the phone volume control is on and potted up, the microphone is on too. EVEN WHEN THE MICROPHONE LIGHT IS OFF! OhmyGosh!

Not only had our radio listeners heard my 2 minutes of frantic screaming and cussing. They also heard me arguing with our office gal about whether my mic was on. But they only heard my side, which made it sound like I was yelling at myself.

The commotion in the control room eventually died down but I was a mess. Slumped over in a puddle of tears and convinced that would be my last radio show. EVER!

Our manager sat me down for a meeting, and as you might expect I received a good 'talking to'. And a one day suspension from work with no pay.

I was sooo embarrassed.

And to this day I have NEVER cussed around a microphone.

On a more serious note: When I lived in Victoria I worked for 100.3 the Q, and every year the radio station was a part of the "Tour de Rock" fundraiser. It was a bike tour of police officers who rode from the northern tip of the island down to Victoria.

The cyclists stopped in towns along the way, raising awareness and money for kids living with cancer. I met so many brave, wonderful people and heard many incredible stories of survival. Those are radio moments I will never, ever forgot.

My family lost my Oma to cancer in 2000. It was a HUGE loss for all of us and I am going to dedicate my part of this book to my Oma, Martha Wahl. I miss you and we think of you all the time. XXX000. Lex

LIANNE YOUNG

THE NEW 1031 FRESH FM LONDON, ONTARIO
WWW.1031FRESHFM.COM

Lianne was born and raised in Oakville, Ontario, but moved out west to attend UBC for Human Kinetics. One day in class she caught herself daydreaming about working in radio, so she switched to the Broadcasting program at Columbia Academy.

In 2001, Lianne was offered a job as an airborne traffic reporter in Vancouver. She worked in a few other markets including Williams Lake, BC and Chatham, Ontario, before she found her current home at The New 1031 Fresh FM in London.

Lianne loves radio: it's spontaneous and immediate. According to Lianne, "It's one take and that's it. You either nail it or you screw it up. The moment passes so quickly, and you move forward. That's radio!"

MY MOM

This story is not about a listener, or an embarrassing radio moment. I'm writing about something that happened off the air several years ago, over 4000 kilometres from my hometown.

It was July 4th, 2002, roughly three weeks into my

radio career when my mom died of breast cancer.

She was the strongest woman you've ever met. She was amazing and I'm proud to call her 'mom'.

She was first diagnosed in her early 30's, not long after I was born. For 20 years she was fine then her cancer came back. But no matter what she was going through, my mom still wanted to be there for me.

When I received my first radio job offer, we sat up on the phone all night, weighing the pros and cons. She was tired and I know she was in pain. But she still wanted to help me. That's what moms do.

My mom lived in Ontario but she had encouraged me to take my first radio job in BC. I was excited about my new career but I hated that I was living across the country.

It was 6 weeks later that I got the news that she was in the hospital and I flew home that day. If necessary, I would have quit my job to be by mom's side but my boss was flexible and very compassionate. Not only did I leave my brand new job for 2 weeks to be with my sister and my father, I was assured I had a job to come back to.

My mom died on the long weekend in July and I remember everything so clearly. Mom and I spent a few moments together before she said goodbye. She lost her battle with cancer on July 4th, 2004. I was 26.

On a personal note, when I was asked to be part of this book I jumped at the chance. I love that we're raising money for breast cancer. We need to raise awareness as well. Thank you for buying this book, thank you for reading these stories and THANK YOU for helping women across the country defeat this monstrous disease.

KAREN DANIELS

JR FM VANCOUVER, BC
WWW.JRFM.COM

Karen Daniels feels like she's been in radio forever, mainly because she can't remember doing anything else. Let's just say it's been more than twenty years in the business.

Her resume looks like a Greyhound bus schedule, with stops in Lloydminster, Regina, Kamloops, Vancouver, Kelowna, Calgary and back to Vancouver, where she currently hosts the morning show at JR FM.

Karen admits she can't do anything else because she doesn't want to actually work for a living. Plus there are so many perks. Radio is fresh, spontaneous, immediate, and there's always lots of free stuff.

According to Karen, the "fun part of radio is the listeners reaction when they meet you for the first time. It's either 'Wow you look a lot better than your picture on the website', or 'You're a lot smaller than you sound on the radio'. Karen still hasn't figured out how to respond to either statement.

ME AND HOTLIPS

The following are not necessarily any of my better moments, but they will live on in radio infamy. For example, my early morning catfight with Hotlips Houlihan.

It was sometime in the late nineties. I was working at a now defunct radio station in Calgary where we had agreed to interview the former MASH star. She was in town doing a small 'one woman show' that our station was promoting.

Hotlips arrived at the station minutes before the interview. As we were sitting down in the studio getting ready to go on I asked her about her time on MASH, and she quickly muttered something back. To be honest I was just putting on my headphones and I didn't catch anything she said.

As soon as we were live I introduced her, and immediately made a reference to her MASH days. After all that's what she's famous for.

To my total shock she called me a name. Live. On air. I don't recall exactly what she called me. A weasel maybe? I leaned over my microphone stand and shot her a look that said "What's your problem, lady?"

My co-host and I proceeded to ask her several questions mainly about MASH, but she was so nasty with her responses that we cut the interview short.

And then complete chaos. When we turned the microphones off she lost it! She said she gave very strict instructions about how she wouldn't discuss her time on Mash. I told her we never got that information.

She basically called me a liar. WHAT? You're calling me out in my own house?

At that point I lost my temper and tossed out a comment about how she hasn't done anything else that anyone would care about. That's when the claws came out.

To my amazement, she reached over and grabbed my sweater, stretching it out of shape. I tried to push her away but she kept grabbing at my sweater.

My co-host attempted to intervene, trying to steer her out the door. But not before she put a hole in my sweater.

I still can't believe it today. One woman show, indeed!

I DID IT FOR CHARITY

My very first radio job was at CKSA in Lloydminster. Like most radio stations, we tried to do as much as possible for the community and local charities.

It was 1980 something and I was the only female on the air at the time. When the local firefighters and police asked me to join them in a charity swimming event, I didn't even hesitate.

It wasn't until later that I realized: 1) I can't really swim, and 2) I'd need to wear a bathing suit in front of the entire town. I couldn't decide which was worse.

To my surprise the day was a huge success. Until the very last race. It was me vs. the one other guy in the pool. Everyone was standing around the pool's edge, cheering their favourite swimmer on to victory.

It was close race and the crowd was going wild. Yelling and screaming their hearts out. I don't wanna brag, but everyone seemed to be cheering for little ol' me!

And as I climbed out of the pool I realized why.

My bikini top had fallen off several lengths ago!

CRISTY BEGGS

HOT 93 FM SASKATOON, SASKATCHEWAN
WWW.HOT93.COM

Cristy started her radio career at Hot 93 in July 1999. She has worked almost every shift at the station, starting with the overnight show. Cristy is now the co-host of the morning show, and she has also worked in the Promotions Department with Hot 93 and sister stations, CJWW and Magic 98.3.

Here are some facts to give you a better idea who Cristy is: If she could meet anyone in the world it would be Ashley Judd - somebody, give that girl an Oscar already!
If she were a superhero, she'd have the ability to read minds, travel by thought, and make things happen by snapping her fingers and wiggling her nose.
Her first car was a red, soft top, 1994 Geo Tracker 4x4. "On paper it sounds tough, but actually it was a glorified golf cart that rolled like a ball!"
In 10 years she'll be... "Probably watching my much younger cousins get married...before I do!"

RELAY FOR LIFE

I work in Saskatoon at a group of three radio stations: HOT 93, CJWW and Magic 98.3. For years we have been the official media sponsors of the Saskatoon "Relay For Life" for the Canadian Cancer Society.

Several years ago, my on air co-host and I came up with a promotion to raise money for the Relay. Every good promo needs a name so we called it "Bald & Blue": if we raised a certain amount of money by a certain date we would go "Bald & Blue" at the Relay. Warren, my co-host at the time had to shave his head bald, and I would dye my long brunette hair, blue. Bright blue. Smurf blue.

We raised the cash (thanks in part to my relatives eager to see me go "blue"). And on the day of Relay, Warren had his head shaved on the event stage, and I spent the day at a local hair salon.

I don't think I've ever sat still for so long. It took 7 hours, a ton of bleach and some bright blue hair dye to go from dark brunette to bright blue, but I loved it! I wore my smurfy blue hair with pride.

I didn't even mind that all my bathroom towels turned blue when I dried my hair. Eventually my shampoo and styling products faded the bright blue colour. By the end of my run as a "bluenette", my hair had turned a strange minty green toothpaste shade.

After another trip to Head Office Hair Design, 10 hours, more bleach and some dark brown dye, my stint as Smurfette was over. But I'd definitely do it again to support the Cancer Society.

Maybe someone should dare me!

GIRLS NIGHT OUT

Part of my job as an announcer is to emcee events, including concerts, festivals and cabarets. The latter is where my 'incident' took place. The big annual rodeo was in town and I was asked to emcee the Cowboy's Cabaret.

I got up on stage, welcomed everyone to the party and introduced the band. It was a fantastic night, with loud music and lot's of dancing. The entire crowd was having a great time, especially my little group. I was feeling no pain and I don't mind telling you I was looking pretty sassy: hot leather pants and a sexy little black shirt that had one long sleeve and left one arm bare. Needless to say, a strapless bra was in order.

At one point during the night, a great two-steppin' song started and this cute cowboy came over and asked me to dance. You betcha! I'm not bad on the dance floor, but this cowboy could really shake it. He had some fancy moves. I was just trying to keep up.

I was a little nervous when he told me to bend over, put my hands between my legs and follow his lead. Ummm - ok. Without missing a beat he bent over me, grabbed my arms, and in one strong move he somersaulted me over his shoulders. Holy C*&P! Fancy move!

I had never received so much attention on the dance floor. I felt like I was in a western remake of Dirty Dancing. Everyone was checking us out, especially the guys in the crowd. Who knew I was such a great little dancer?

The cowboy finally put me down and we settled into a basic two-step. Within seconds, he began staring at me, then grinning at me …and THEN, apologizing. What the heck?

And it suddenly dawned on me as I slowly followed his gaze down to my shirt. Which was NOT doing its job covering the upper half of my body. During our fancy dance moves, my shirt and bra got a little twisted around. Girls' night out took on a whole new meaning.

And I had been on and off the stage, introducing the bands. I may as well have been wearing a sign on my forehead, advertising who I was and where I worked. Nice.

DENYSE SIBLEY

FX101.9 FM HALIFAX, NOVA SCOTIA
WWW.FX1019.CA

Denyse Sibley has been a favorite with Nova Scotia radio listeners for many years. With her undeniable sense of adventure, Denyse brings edge and spice to FX101.9's popular morning show.

A farmer's daughter, Denyse was born and raised in the Musquodoboit Valley, where she now lives with her own family. This mom on the move has run several marathons for the Arthritis Society and has recently became a certified personal trainer.

Along with family, fitness and FM radio, Denyse can be proud of her airborne accomplishments. She has been a pilot since 1997, and serves on the Debert Flight Centre's Board of Directors. Denyse has accompanied such flight teams as the US Navy's Blue Angels, and has even been skydiving a time or two.

JUST SLIDE BEHIND THE WHEEL

I remember one beautiful spring afternoon I was on location at O'Regans, a Halifax car dealership. I was all decked out in my black leather pants, ready to sell some hot new sports cars for the upcoming summer season.

I am a proud Corvette owner, so the sales associates really wanted me to slide behind the wheel of one of the hot new 'vettes. So me (and my tight leather pants) crawled into a flashy yellow one.

I did my next 60 second cut in live from behind the steering wheel of this gorgeous car, which was nestled in the showroom beside my broadcast booth. I finished the on air cut-in and crawled back out, happy I could accommodate our client.

Later that afternoon the receptionist pulled me aside, asking if I had a long coat or a sweater. Huh? Why?

Turns out that when I was sliding out of the yellow 'vette, I managed to rip the bum right out of my leather pants. I was FLASHING MY HOT PINK PANTIES to everyone in the showroom!

How many laps did I make around the dealership that afternoon, with my radio station nametag hanging off the front of my shirt and my hot pink panties peeking out the back of my pants?

SAM COOK

COUNTRY 95.3 TORONTO, ONTARIO
WWW.COUNTRY953.COM

Sam Cook is the weekend Diva at Country 95.3 in Toronto. In addition to her love affair with radio, Sam is very passionate about acting. She attended Mohawk College in Hamilton where she graduated from TV Broadcasting. During her final semester, Sam went to New York City where she interned for The Late Show With David Letterman as the segment producer for the Stupid Human and Pet Tricks.

Sam is also an actress who has appeared in many commercials, films and television series including the hit show "UHOH" which was featured on YTV and on several stations in Australia and Singapore.

In the spring of 2006, Sam began her own entertainment company called Angel Wing Entertainment. You can check out the website at www.angelwingentertainment.com.

FRIENDS

I love my job and I love meeting my listeners. I'd like to think I have a great relationship with them, and I hope they view me as a friend.

And friends talk. Sometimes when my listeners call up the station, they talk to me about VERY personal things going on in their lives. Radio is very unusual that way - we develop relationships with people we've never met. Think about it... if you listen to someone every single day for a few hours, you feel like you know them pretty well.

A few years ago I received a late night phone call on the request line. It was a young girl who I used to chat with every few weeks. She was about 14 years old. I had never actually met her before; she was just a voice on the phone. I think she was kind of a loner. And maybe a little lonely.

Less than a minute into the phone call she started to cry. Things turned serious very quickly.

Being a teenager had gotten the best of her and she admitted to me that she used a piece of broken glass to cut herself. She was bleeding heavily and no one was home. After she saw the blood she was shocked back into reality. She wanted to live. And now she was scared.

The only person she could think of to turn to for help was me. Her friend.

My heart dropped. What do I do? This young girl I've never even met, was calling ME for help. I didn't even know her full name, never mind where she lived.

The reality of the situation was that I still had a full show to do. I took a breath and thought, 'OK, I have two choices, play the music and continue with the show OR let the computer take over the show (in auto), possibly get yelled at by my boss, but try save this young girl's life'.

Of course, I chose the latter.

She was slowly fading away, barely mumbling to me now. I had to keep her conscious until she told me her address. The second I got it from her, I dialled the police on another line and explained the situation. And all the while I stayed on the phone and kept my teenage friend talking, right up until I heard the sound of sirens in the background.

When the police and paramedics took over from her end, I finally hung up. But I was really rattled.

It's been over 5 years since I've spoken to my young friend, though she recently sent me an email. She's all grown up now and has a baby girl of her own. I'm just happy she had a chance to grow up.

She thanked me for saving her life.

And being a friend.

SUE DEYELL

Q107 CALGARY, ALBERTA
WWW.Q107FM.CA

Sue began her radio career in 1993, days after she graduated from Seneca College School of Communication Arts in Toronto. She has worked at stations in Brockville, Kingston and Moncton before landing in Calgary at her current home, Q107 FM.

Over the years, Sue has had the chance to meet and interview many amazing people: Olympians, pro athletes, authors and actors.

She's also seen more than her share if great concerts: AC/DC, The Rolling Stones, Sting and many more. A couple of Sue's favourite musicians are Melissa Etheridge & Billy Idol. She met Melissa backstage at a concert in Vancouver in 1990, and says, "Melissa was super nice and signed a glass window for me that I sat with throughout the concert, then later had framed. It's proudly hanging on my wall to this day!" About Billy, Sue says, "I met Billy Idol backstage at a show in Calgary, and got my picture taken with him. There we are, both of us sneering at the camera in typical 'Billy' style. Except he looks a lot cooler than me!

According to Sue, "Through radio, I've been lucky enough to see this beautiful country, meet some wonderful people and be part of a business like no other. Getting up at 3:30am is a chore sometimes, but I can't imagine myself doing anything else!"

MEMORIES – GOOD AND BAD

I still clearly remember the first time I ever got up on stage to introduce a band. I'd never been so terrified in my life. In fact, I was convinced that I would throw up and make a complete fool of myself. Today, I still get a sick feeling in my stomach when I have to get up on stage in front of a huge crowd, but it's a lot less now – and afterwards I generally remember what I said.

Some of the funniest moments of my career were "behind the mic", so that listeners didn't really know what was happening. I remember a 7-minute newscast at my very first job in Brockville, Ontario. I worked with a lot of nuts, who thought it would be fun to try and get me to laugh during my cast.

Keep in mind my news mic was in a teeny little news booth just outside the on air studio. The moment I started my newscast my three co-workers (three guys) all crawled into my news booth on their hands and knees. One of my co-workers crawled under my chair and proceeded to lick my leg, while the other two played with my hair, stuck their fingers in my ears and generally did all they could to make me crack. Radio has changed a LOT since then, especially in the bigger cities. But I'm sure there are a few small town stations out there where these things still happen.

The other silly moment I recall was a lot more painful. The guys I worked with on the morning show were playing soccer in the control room with one of those big exercise balls. Yes, during my newscast! One of my cohorts kicked the ball, and it slammed into the back of my head. The force caused my forehead to smash into my microphone, which promptly came unhooked and dropped loudly onto my desk in front of me!

Rubbing my head and straightening my now crooked glasses, I picked up my mic and giggled through the rest of my newscast – with the boys screaming with laughter from the floor beside me. We were all so mature back then!

It's been my pleasure over the years to work with many announcers whose main goal in life was to crack up their fellow announcers on air. Since the "leg licking episode" most have failed, but some have certainly succeeded. Cheers to them! And I bet it's never occurred to you those silly things actually happen in the control room when your favourite announcer is on air.

I feel very lucky to have succeeded in radio. It certainly has its ups and downs, but it's also the most fulfilling job in the world. Over the years I've had marriage proposals, flowers sent to me, and professions of love – which, once you get over the creepiness of it all, makes me realize just how lucky I am.

I have a job where people (hopefully) want to listen to what I have to say, laugh at my jokes, and enjoy me just being me. I'm honoured to talk to them every morning. Man, I love my job!

ERIN DAVIS

98.1 CHFI TORONTO, ONTARIO
WWW.CHFI.COM

Erin has been a fixture on the Canadian radio landscape for over 20 years. In 2002, she was named the year's first Chatelaine Woman Of Influence, joining the ranks of such luminaries as Kim Campbell, Roberta Bondar and Pamela Wallin.

In the summer of 2003, Erin saw a lifelong dream come true when the W Network called and offered her the opportunity to host her own live national tv talk show, W Live with Erin Davis. Around the same time she also made her live theatre debut as the Fairy Godmother in "Cinderella" at Toronto's historic Elgin Theatre for a month long run.

In March of 2006, she was the Grand Marshal of the 2006 Toronto St. Patrick's Day Parade, and in April, Erin was honoured to be named 2006 Woman of the Year at the Toronto Consumers Choice Awards.

Erin's charitable works are numerous. She is a regular co-host on the Easter Seals Telethon on CBC television and is a supporter of North York General Hospital. Erin is very active with the Canadian Breast Cancer Foundation and has also worked with the Children's Wish Foundation, for which she raised an astounding $160,000 in the summer of 1998, *simply by shaving her head (thanks to the generosity of CHFI listeners).*

IT AIN'T EASY BEIN' GREEN

I have a bazillion stories - some inspiring, some funny, some just amusing. But here's one that I tell whenever we have a round of "can you believe we were ever that GREEN?"

It was April of 1982. Just sprung from Loyalist College, I had a job waiting for me at CFRA, the #1 radio station in Ottawa. It would be my second full-time job, having worked at an easy-listening station in Belleville, while also earning my 2-year broadcasting certificate.

At the tender age of 19, I was ready to take on the world. Apparently the world wasn't quite ready for me; News Director Steve Madely told me that I'd have to work a month of overnights, to get used to the real world of a bustling morning newsroom. Only I'd be seeing it from the night side; my job was clearing off the news printers, and doing whatever else it took to get the city's top news team in shape for the morning ahead.

It was my first shift. I drove from my rented apartment in Nepean to the CFRA studios downtown in the Nation's Capital. I was nervous as anyone starting a new job. And eager to make a good first impression.

I was doing my research and listening to the CFRA evening show, hosted by dj Mark Elliot. He played some great top 40 tunes, and then I heard him tease who was coming up. Thank goodness I had been listening. Now it would seem like I really HAD been doing my homework.

My little Dodge Colt found its way to a parking spot,

and I made my way into the building. I remembered how to get to the newsroom - if I hadn't, the persistent clatter and hum of printers from the wire services would have led the way. Upon entering, I saw a young, blond man reading over some news stories. He must be the evening news guy that Mark Elliot had just been talking about on air.

"Hi there," I said, putting on my most confident voice. I strode across the newsroom, hand out and ready to shake his. "I'm Erin. You must be Huey!" He gave me a puzzled look. "Oh, I'm sorry," I responded, realizing I'd made a mistake. "I thought you were Huey Lewis?"

With that, a smile crept across his face, and a sick feeling crept into my stomach. I realized I'd really missed the mark. "Why would you think that?" he asked.

"Well, I was listening to the radio on the drive here. Mark Elliot said, 'Coming up, Huey Lewis, and the news.' I assumed you did the evening newscasts?"

As he - and then both of us - dissolved into laughter, my new friend introduced himself as Steve Winogron, and proceeded to explain to me exactly who Huey Lewis and The News were.

It was pretty funny.

But I still felt like an idiot.

KELSI JORDAN

COUNTRY 105 FM CALGARY, ALBERTA
WWW.COUNTRY105.COM

Kelsi Jordan got her first radio job in 1990 and has worked at stations in Nelson, Vernon, and Kelowna, BC, and Medicine Hat and Drumheller, Alberta. In 1995, Kelsi accepted a job at Country 105 in Calgary. Eleven years later they can't seem to get rid of her. She hosts the drive home show with her pal, Roger Rhodes.

Radio has been an incredible experience. Kelsi has met some big names like the Dixie Chicks and Keith Urban. In 2003 she was honored by Calgary Tourism as the 'Media Person of the Year'.

Kelsi has a ton of embarrassing 'radio' stories and quickly decided to ask female announcers across Canada to share their memories as well. This collection became "I'M NOT WEARING PANTS, True tales from Canadian Radio Gals". After a cancer scare in 2005, Kelsi decided to donate a portion of the proceeds to breast cancer.

"WHAT DO RADIO ANNOUNCERS DO DURING THE SONGS? DO YOU JUST SIT THERE?"

That's a question we hear a lot. We do a million things after we introduce the song. We answer listener questions on the phone. We record and edit phone calls to play on the air. We keep track of the commercials and the music. We plan our contests, weather and traffic breaks. Sometimes we race to the bathroom.

There are a lot of scary bathroom stories in radio. My life changing bathroom event was at a small radio station in British Columbia, my first real radio job. During the evening show I zipped out to the bathroom, did my business and raced back, only to find the studio door was jammed shut. I was locked out and we were OFF the air for almost an hour!

I was actually fired from that job, but not for that. A few months later I was on kitchen duty and my boss saw me doing the dishes during my show. I had also scrubbed out that disgusting layer of grease from the microwave, taken out the garbage and watered the dying spider plants. As it turns out, the boss did not appreciate my domestic skills.

I was just pulling the drain from the sink and wiping my hands when I turned around to see his big red face inches from my nose, yelling "WHO THE HELL IS ON THE AIR?" A stunned silence came over the radio station. "Dead air" silence. My song was over. Along with my job. But the kitchen was sparkling!

Last year I read that on average, radio announcers get fired at least six times through out their career. Only five more to go...

WHERE EVERYBODY KNOWS YOUR NAME

The great thing about being on air is that people know your name. And the downside of being on air is that people know your name.

A few months ago I had an infection and had to go to a clinic to get some tests done. I must have gotten stage fright because for whatever reason, I couldn't give a pee sample. The nurse was very sweet, and just told me to drop it off the next morning. She even gave me my own pee cup to take home.

I had to run some errands the following day - the bank, the shoe store, Home Depot. I finally made it to the medical clinic where to my total horror, I discovered I had lost my pee sample! I searched all my bags, my purse, and my briefcase. NO PEE SAMPLE!

You've seen them before. A clear plastic bottle with a bright orange cap and a label with your name written on it in HUGE black letters. I never did find it, though I have a feeling I took it out of my bag at Home Depot, when I grabbed my wallet and my paint chip colour. My pee sample bottle with the bright orange lid

Clearly labelled with my full name. Accck!

"DO RADIO ANNOUNCERS GET STALKERS?"

I had this one guy who used to send me pumpkins. One pumpkin a week for over a year. I live in Canada… where do you even GET pumpkins in February? I never found out who he was and one week he just stopped. I hope he's okay but I don't miss the pumpkins.

I'm making light of the stalker thing, but it's actually pretty creepy. I was at a charity event with a tv gal one night, and we started comparing stalkers. Turns out we were getting spooky love-notes from the same guy … he was just changing our names and descriptions in the letter. A stalker "form" letter.

We have the Chief of Police on our radio show every once in awhile. He's an awesome guy, and very witty. I met him when he was a Staff Sergeant, and he actually caught 2 of my stalkers. I wanted to send him a thank you card, but I couldn't find one for that particular occasion. Hallmark, are you listening?

If someone spooky is ever following you home, here's a great tip I learned from the cops. DO NOT GO HOME! Drive straight to a fire hall, block the driveway with your car and lean on your horn like a 5 alarm fire until the guys run out to rescue you.

You'll turn the tables on the creep following you and you could meet some sexy firemen as a bonus. Although if you do this too many times at the same fire station, they'll red flag you. Then the guys following you home will be police and psychiatrists!

My most recent "follow me home" story was definitely the spookiest one of my entire career. The stalker in question was an attractive older man, obviously the successful, executive type. Nice suit, trendy shades, new silver SUV, etc.

He pulled up beside my car out of nowhere. He was giving me that "Hel-LO" look with his eyes. You know that "look" some dudes have. Actually I couldn't really tell for sure if he was giving me the "look" because he was wearing shades, but I'm sure he was.

Anyway, he's smirking at me, tossing me a sexy little wave. I try to ignore him. He keeps waving and mouthing "hi!" I continue ignoring him and speed up. He speeds up too, which is when I start getting a little paranoid.

Suddenly he rolls down his window, leans out of the

car a bit and throws out a devilish grin. He's an attractive fellow, but it's been a long day and by this time I'm freaked out and fed up. I give him a rude one fingered gesture and slam on my breaks to slide into the left turn lane.

He sails by me staring into his rear view mirror with an astonished look on his face. "What a jerk," I think to myself. "Probably can't believe he struck out!"

The next day we get a call in the studio from the Big Cheese, Garry McKenzie. He's the General Manager of our radio group. My boss's boss.

A successful, attractive, executive type. Who drives a new silver SUV. Who was in the vehicle next to me on the drive home yesterday and was trying to say hi.

Who I DID wave to.

Sort of.

KELLY GRANT

Z95.3 VANCOUVER, BC
WWW.Z95.COM

Kelly's career began in 1997, cleaning out community cruisers for a radio station at age 17. She was determined to get her foot in the door somehow. Kelly has worked at six radio stations through out her career: starting in Duncan, BC and then five different stations in Vancouver.

Kelly Grant loves radio: her station, her co-workers, her listeners and the cool people she's met along the way, including Shaggy ("what a flirt"), Pamela Anderson ("she's very teeny"), and Chad Kroeger ("the personification of a rock star").

Kelly labels herself a radio 'junkie'. She says, "every day is different and every day is a challenge. It's the most fulfilling, fun, and oddly stressful (but most rewarding) gig around."

ME AND HOWIE D.

Do you remember being a teenager in love? Seeing that boy you liked in the hall, exchanging a few words, then walking away and not remembering a single thing that came out of your mouth?

I had that experience a few years ago, and I

wasn't a teenager. At age 25, I caught myself giggling like a schoolgirl when I interviewed Howie D of the Backstreet Boys.

I'm a little embarrassed to admit this, but I have been a fan of the Backstreet Boys since I was a teenager. I grew up listening to them on the radio and seeing them on tv, and I was totally pumped about this interview.

I was given a total of 10 minutes to chat with Howie D and I was just over the moon. I could actually feel myself blushing as soon as I saw him. He walked right up to me and introduced himself (like I didn't already know who he was).

I wiped the sweat off my hands in case he reached out to shake them. And then I followed him to the guys' dressing room. Of course all I could think was, 'Ohmigawd, I'm in the Backstreet Boys' dressing room'.

I could hardly concentrate because all their personal stuff was lying around the room; magazines, shoes, Vicks cold medication. In my head I was working up a little fantasy starring Howie D and that Vicks Vapour Rub ... ehem – oops, I think he just said something. I better start paying attention!

During the interview all the other guys kept wandering in and out of the room: first Nick, then Kevin. And then I spotted A.J. in my peripheral vision. He was getting a neck massage in the corner of the room. His eyes were closed and he was smiling. Yummy.

I'm supposed to be a professional, but I honestly don't recall anything about that interview or a single question I asked him. I do remember all the little fantasies in my head but I couldn't go to air with those!

When I got back to the station I listened to the interview, hearing my questions for what felt like the first time. Turns out the chemistry between Howie and I was great - not romantic, dammit, but very friendly.

And what a flashback to my teen years: I'd never want to go back to them, but for ten minutes with a Backstreet Boy, I'll gladly channel them.

TARA DAWN WINSTONE

B101 BARRIE, ONTARIO
WWW.B101FM.COM

Brampton, Ontario native Tara Dawn Winstone began her radio career at age 12, when her mom had asked her to make a tape of her favourite music for those long commutes to work. Tara coerced her pals to help record a full variety show on cassette. The final 90 minute tape contained a total of 84 minutes of non-stop entertainment and a whopping 6 minutes of music!

After graduating from the Broadcasting program at Humber College in '94, Tara was hired by Barrie's B101fm where she still works today.

Tara is also host of the local news show for Roger's Television and a reality-style documentary series called "A Day in the Life".

RADIO LESSON #1 – THEATRE OF THE MIND

One of the most embarrassing radio moments happened my first year in the business. My boss had asked me to broadcast live from the local mall to benefit the Children of Chernobyl.

I was actually on location for two reasons: to help get the word out for the charity and also to help them sell their new mascot, the Willy. Willy was a cute, furry toy ferret. When you prodded him with a stick he would crawl all over you.

Remember it was my first year in radio. I was pretty nervous, and even more so when I realized we wouldn't be taping the cut-ins. Everything would be live.

As soon as I reached the mall I grabbed the older man in charge of the fundraiser, along with one of the stuffed ferrets (Willy) and began doing my report.

Me: "Thank you for joining us Mr. Cox. Can you tell us about your Willy?"

Mr. Cox: "Glad to be here Tara...but I think it would be better if I showed you what Willy can do." He placed the little toy on my arm.

Me: "Ohhhh – (giggle, giggle) it feels funny...kind of ticklish but soft."

Mr. Cox: "I know. And if you poke Willy with this stick, it will start to jump around on it's own."

Me: "OOOOh...(tee hee)...that's amazing! I wish I had one!"

Mr. Cox: "Well you've come to the right place young lady. For only $20, you can have a Willy of your own to play with and all money raised will go to help the Children of Chernobyl!"

Me: "Wow...that is a deal! Thank you for joining us Mr. Cox. Let's hope you sell a lot of your Willy's today."

After a brief wrap up, I sent it back to our afternoon guy in the studio. But I was greeted with dead air. Oh-oh. What happened to our connection?

I tried to throw it back to the station again. Nothing.

"Hey there." Nervous giggle. "Uh hum... Back to you, Jim."

Finally our afternoon guy responded. But it was clear that he was having trouble speaking. He almost sounded like he was choking.

After a few failed attempts at spitting out whatever he was trying to say he gave up and sent it over to the news centre. Once again we were greeted with silence.

A few more seconds of dead air and Jim went straight into music.

I was a little confused, but I didn't think much of it until I got back to the station and Jim gleefully played the tape back for me.

As you can imagine I was truly mortified. There I was going on and on about Mr. Cox and his Willy.

NATASHA RAPCHUK

AM 770 CHQR CALGARY, ALBERTA
WWW.AM770CHQR.COM

Natasha Rapchuk is the News Director for Corus Radio Calgary. After graduating with a Bachelor of Journalism degree from Carleton University in Ottawa, Natasha moved back to her home province of Alberta. She got her start working at small, rural radio stations in Hinton and Wetaskawin.

Natasha finally got her "big break" in 1999, getting hired for evening and weekend news on CHQR news/talk/sports in Calgary. She worked her way up the news ladder, and now heads up the Corus Calgary newsroom that includes seven full-timers and three part-timers.

Natasha works long hours, but loves her job. She has a total passion for news and current events. And she also knows there's nothing like breaking a huge story, or covering a live news event, and bringing the answers to her CHQR listeners.

AND NOW... THE NEWS

Okay, I admit it. I do get the odd raised eyebrow, or other surprised reaction when someone phones for the news director and hears my female voice on the line.

("Huh? You're the news DIRECTOR?") But nowadays it's not as uncommon as it was ten years ago to have a female in a managerial position in the newsroom.

People often ask how I can get through an entire newscast with that serious "news" tone.

My main trick for avoiding on-air giggling fits is to think of something really sad or sombre. I'll think about one of the stories I'm about to read that is very sad, such as a fatal hurricane, or bombings in Iraq. I know it sounds morbid, but that way I'll remember that it's important to maintain decorum and seriousness and show respect.

I very rarely get emotional reading sad stories on air. There is a certain amount of detachment you have to develop working in a newsroom, otherwise you'd be an emotional wreck at the end of the day.

And now I'll tell you a story that goes against everything I've just said. It's from my early days doing news on the morning show at Power 107 FM Calgary. I can laugh about it now, but at the time I really thought I might lose my job.

You may have noticed that news or weather reports on the radio are usually sponsored by a certain company or business. In radio we call these ads "sponsor credits", and they are usually read live on-air by the news announcer at the beginning of the cast. For example, "Power 107 News is brought to you by Harry's Hot Tubs, in business over 40 years".

Being the conscientious newsperson that I am, I usually read all my sponsor credits *before* I go on air, just to make sure they make sense. Thank goodness I read this one beforehand. I knew right off the top this little monster was going to cause me trouble.

The ad was for a chain of pet stores, promoting a new product that allowed your dog to 'carry his own poop'.

That was exactly how it was worded. "So your dog can carry his own poop!" The product was some sort of little bag that ties on to your dog's leash.

"Poop" is not necessarily a funny word, but I don't use it in everyday conversation. And I NEVER say it on the radio. I'm supposed to be a respected newsperson! But I suddenly got a mental picture in my head of this cute little wiener dog scooping up after himself and carrying around his own poop bag. I could feel the laughter starting in the pit of my tummy, but I tried to hold it inside while I began my newscast.

"Good morning. At 7:30, it's minus 5 in Calgary. I'm Natasha Rapchuck with Power 107 News, brought to you by -..."

THAT'S when I lost it.

I still had the little doggie visual in my head, and I couldn't believe I had to say the word 'poop'. It started with the giggles but soon I was laughing so hard, I was crying. Live. On the air at 7:30 in the morning! And giggling is contagious. Soon the three dj's in the studio were all laughing too.

Fortunately this was a Top 40 FM morning show, so the atmosphere was pretty loose. I think it took me three tries to get through the 'poop' credit. It was a nightmare. The rest of the newscast was pretty much a blur.

I really thought I was going to get into trouble with my bosses but they were very understanding. And the listeners thought this whole thing was hilarious. Especially for a serious newsperson like myself to crack up over the word 'poop'. One guy called in to say he almost drove off the road he was laughing so hard at ME laughing so hard!

In addition, the marketing director for the pet store found it so amusing, he played the tape of my laughing fit for the company's board of directors. The whole fiasco generated more attention to their product, and they were thrilled!

Since then I've taught myself a few more mental tricks to avoid on-air laughing fits, and I'm thankful to say it's never happened again. But every once in awhile, when I see a dog, I imagine it carrying around it's own poop.

And of course, I giggle.

CAROL THOMSON

MAGIC 98.3 SASKATOON, SASKATCHEWAN
WWW.MAGIC983.FM

Carol graduated from Lethbridge Community College and worked at radio stations in Prince Albert, Medicine Hat and Calgary, before settling down at Magic 98.3 in Saskatoon.

She loves her job, especially the people she works with, describing them as "creative, funny and sometimes downright odd". Because of radio, Carol has also had experiences that she may not have had otherwise: including scuba diving, parachuting and harness racing!

Carol says radio is like a member of the family. In her words, "We wake up to the radio – we drive with it. It informs us. It entertains. And sometimes it drives us crazy. Just like a real family."

"CAN SOMEONE GET THE DOOR?"

Picture it... my very first week in radio. I was working an evening shift, and I barely knew my way around the studio, never mind the entire radio station. I had received a call from someone wanting to drop something off after hours. The control room didn't actually have any windows looking outside, and I couldn't see the street to watch for this guy.

Hmm... what should I do? This was back in the days of albums and 45's, so I put on a longer tune and found a side door off the control room that entered into a rundown hallway. The upstairs led to seedy apartments of ill repute. The exterior door led to the street, and from there I could see the main doors and watch for the man who had called.

I didn't want to miss the end of my song on the air so I rushed out the side door to find this dude and grab his package. So to speak.

The next few moments were in slow motion. As the door was whooshing shut I realized, THERE WAS NO DOORKNOB ON THE OTHER SIDE! I was locked out of the building on a Friday night when nobody else was around to let me back in! And I was on the air!

What happened next was like something out of a really bad horror movie. After scratching desperately at the door, I kicked it a few times to vent my frustration. In a panic I ran upstairs to the seedy apartments. I was flailing my arms, running up and down the halls when suddenly a man popped out of a doorway, whiskey bottle in hand, and asked me what was wrong.

In any spooky horror movie this would have been the creepy guy stuck in the time warp. His dark hair was greased back in 50's style and he was actually wearing a dirty plaid suit! He asked me if I wanted to call someone from inside his apartment. I hesitated, but knew at that moment my song was definitely over, and all anyone could hear on the air was the "ca-chuk, ca-chuk" of the needle, at the end of the record.

I cautiously entered his apartment and was halfway to the phone when I realized that the only phone number

I knew was for the control room. THAT I WAS LOCKED OUT OF!

Somehow in my panic I also remembered my boss's last name and tried to reach him, but he was at the lake for the weekend. Probably a good thing under the circumstances.

I left 'spooky plaid' man and his weird apartment, raced down the back stairs and out the door into the alley. I had one last hope. The back door is never open. What are the odds it would be open that night?

Someone must have been watching over me because the second I grasped the doorknob I knew it wasn't locked. I flew into the control room to find the newsperson standing there in shock not knowing what to do. The off air alarm was blaring. I shut off the alarm, started up the next song, and blurted that I had been locked out.

He just walked out of the room in silence. He was probably thinking what I was thinking. "She's history. Fired for sure, probably by Monday!" But as I mentioned earlier, the boss was at the lake. He never found out about any of it. Getting locked out of the building. Spooky plaid man. Being off the air. None of it!

And all these years later, I'm still working in radio.

But now whenever I exit an unknown door, I always check to see there's a doorknob on the other side.

SHELBY GRAYSON

100.3 THE Q VICTORIA, BC
WWW.THEQ.FM

Shelby began her radio career in 1997. She's worked at stations in Kamloops, Kelowna and Regina, and Shelby is now home at the highly rated 100.3 the Q, in Victoria.

It's hard to pinpoint what Shelby loves most about radio, but her top three list would include: the connection she's built with her listeners; the music she plays; and of course, the free stuff!

According to Shelby, "Every day is different. I get to be creative and best of all, be myself! The diversity of radio fits my personality."

MY FAVOURITE INTERVIEW

Over the years I've had the opportunity to interview a number of artists, both in person and on the phone. The highlight of my interviewing career was when I got the call from Joe Elliot, the lead singer of Def Leppard.

About three weeks earlier we found out that Joe would give us some of his time. I was pretty excited. After all we're talking about the man behind hit songs like: Rock Of Ages, Foolin' and Photograph.

I prepped for hours and when the call was patched through I was shaking all over. Turns out my anxiety was totally unnecessary. I've never had a more relaxed, friendly conversation with a musician before.

Joe answered all my questions and then some. We spoke for about an hour about everything: Def Leppard's start as a young rock band, the band fights, the soft side of the guys that nobody ever saw and Joe's thoughts on them getting inducted into the Rock & Roll Hall of Fame (slim to none in his opinion).

Imagine getting 60 minutes to talk to your favourite musician. And nothing was off limits. I was in heaven.

I could have chatted forever but Joe was finally yanked off the line by their manager to do a sound check. Damn.

The voice behind one of the biggest rock bands in the world turned out to be one of the most humble and gracious men I've ever met.

I got home from the station that day, and I still could not get over the fact that today at "work" I talked to Joe Elliot for an hour.

TAMMY COLE

EZ ROCK 104.9 EDMONTON, ALBERTA
WWW.EZROCK1049.COM

Tammy Cole decided when she grew up she would be either a police officer or a radio announcer. She flipped a coin and radio won.

Tammy settled into her first radio job in 1991, doing overnights at Country 105 in Calgary. From there she moved on to stations in Edson, Hinton and Sudbury, and finally her current position as midday announcer and music director at EZ Rock 104.9 in Edmonton.

Tammy has met some cool people in her career, including Sting, Michael Buble and Alice Cooper, but she admits her favourite thing about being the music director is adding new tunes to the play-list every week. She loves being the first to hear a brand new song and believing in it so much, she'll fight to get it on the air. (She throws what she calls a "Tammy Tantrum".)

Tammy is a Taurus, and a great multi-tasker. She can eat ice cream while riding her stationary bike. And she's famous at the radio station for making S'mores and grilled cheese sandwiches on her office Foreman Grill!

"LADY, STEP AWAY FROM THE SHANAHAN!"

I have always been a willing volunteer when it comes to making a fool out of myself in the interest of a good station promotion.

Which explains why, when I was working in Sudbury, I agreed to participate in a hypnotist performance. I had been hypnotized before and was apparently a good candidate.

For legal reasons, I'll give the hypnotist an alias. Let's call him "the Great Slink-ini". I had been under the Great Slink-ini's spell for about ten minutes before he asked for some fun suggestions from the audience. One of my co-workers yelled out, "tell her she's meeting Brendan Shanahan". (She knew I had a little teeny crush on the NHL player.)

Slink-ini the Hypnotist chose a member of the audience to play the role of Brendan Shanahan. The dude he chose happened to be our radio station producer, who was also hypnotized and sitting beside me on stage.

When the Great Slink-ini told me I was right next to Brendan Shanahan all hell broke lose. Ladies, I'm sure you can appreciate my next moves. I literally threw myself at our producer who I've worked with for years, and tried to rip his shirt off!

Picture yourself doing that to an older gentleman you work with and have to see every day. Not pretty. After it was over I was thoroughly amused and a little embarrassed, but quickly erased the incident from my mind.

A few weeks later a package arrived for me at the station. Inside I found a signed lacrosse program from the real Brendan Shanahan. Apparently an acquaintance of his was in the audience and took great pleasure in recounting my embarrassing "attack" to Brendan himself. I have no idea what he thought but that lacrosse program is one of my most valued possessions.

I've since left that job, to the huge relief of the producer I attacked.

For months afterward he would turn red and barely make eye contact when we passed each other in the hall.

PAM STEVENS

JACK FM VANCOUVER, BC
WWW.JACKFM.COM

Pam began her radio career in 1986. She started in Trail, BC then moved quickly to the major markets of Edmonton and Vancouver, where Pam currently works at Jack FM.

There are many perks in radio and Pam has taken advantage of all the amazing life experiences that radio provides. She's spent over 2500 hours in a Cessna 172 and almost an hour in an F-18. Pam has also hung out with some incredibly cool celebrities like David Bowie, Johnny Cash and Duran Duran.

Confucious say: "When you love what you do you don't work a day in your life." Pam agrees wholeheartedly!

"DON'T I KNOW YOU?"

I began my radio career as most do, under an assumed name. To be honest, my legal surname is German and rarely pronounced correctly on the first try, so I didn't mind when I was asked to pick something else to use on air. I was actually a little thrilled to have an alter ego.

Since I had moved to Vancouver to go to school, I had to set up my new life and find a new dentist, a doctor,

new bank, etc. One of my classmates recommended her family doctor who was a big fan of CKNW, the station that was about to offer me my first radio job as a traffic reporter.

About three years into that gig I was in for my annual physical. The good doctor was in the middle of taking a pap smear, when something about work came up in our conversation.

There I am, feet are in the stirrups, getting cold under that paper blanket, waiting for the whole thing to just be over when my doctor finally puts 2 and 2 together. He rolls back on his stool and exclaims "You're Pam *Stevens*?"

To this day, I can't think of a worse place to be recognized.

CAROL GASS

THE WOLF @ 97 FM PRINCE GEORGE, BC
WWW.97FM.CA

Carol is the morning gal at The Wolf @ 97 FM in Prince George, BC. She's also the Promotions Director. (And the web girl, and the female production voice, etc. etc.) Carol can't actually remember how she got the idea to get into radio, but one day she found herself immersed in college life at BCIT.

Carol loves the creativity that comes with her job. Topping her list of achievements are the three radio plays she's written, cast and produced as part of a huge WOLF promotion.

Carol loves the other perks of radio. She's had the chance to meet country legend, George Jones (and she kissed him on the cheek!) She met Kenny Rogers backstage, after a concert she calls 'One of the Top Ten Concert Experiences of My Life'. Carol has also been on Dwight Yoakam's bus, where she presented him with a pair of underwear. But she's not saying whose.

THE EMCEE

I really love radio, but if I had the guts to work for myself I'd go on the road as a professional emcee. As a result of my radio career, I have emceed everything from "Mr. (fill in the blank)" pageants to Canada Day in the Park, local fashion shows and ritzy "mucky muck" events. It was at one such highbrow function where I suffered another HUGE Carol Gass Gaff.

Early in my radio career I was asked to host the Prince George "Citizen of the Year" event. It's quite a big deal here and all of the wealthy elite make it a priority to attend. I honestly don't know why I was asked to emcee. Possibly the regular host wasn't available. Or maybe they just didn't know me well enough to know how silly I am.

It was a sold out show and everyone was dressed to the nines. The champagne was flowing and the nominees, all prominent members of the community, were nervous. It really was quite the "do."

Before the event I had attended many planning meetings with organizers to make sure the night would go off without a hitch. The gala was progressing beautifully, and I was feeling quite relaxed. Finally it was time to crown the new Citizen of the Year.

I asked the former 'Citizen Of The Year' to come forward to say a few words. As he stepped up to the podium, I gave him a hug and ad-libbed a quick introduction. And just before handing over the microphone I asked, "Do you feel like a queen handing over your tiara?"

I heard the simultaneous gasp from what sounded like everyone in the audience. Then dead silence.

How was I to know that the outgoing "Citizen of the Year" was gay?

AMBER LEE TRUDEAU

VIBE 98.5 FM CALGARY, ALBERTA
WWW.VIBE985.COM

Amber Lee grew up in Edmonton, and started her radio career in 1998 after graduating from the Radio program at NAIT. Her first on air job was in Fort McMurray, Alberta. Amber then moved to major market radio, first Vancouver and now Calgary, where you can hear her on Vibe 98.5.

Amber loves radio because it's immediate and LIVE. It requires you to be creative and think about things in a different light. Radio has also given Amber the chance to meet cool people and experience amazing things. And of course, the free stuff is always great.

I DO, LIVE ON AIR

One of the coolest radio events I have been part of was an on air marriage. We had a contest called 'I Do, I Do with the Zed Morning Crew'. Couples had to email us reasons why they should be married on the air.

The winning couple was notified and everything was arranged a week before the live wedding date. We had the dress, a justice of the peace, flowers, food and a photographer lined up.

On the big day we met at the station at 5am, dressed in our Sunday best. We opened up the studio to the lucky couple, their families and local tv crews. We met the family, heard funny stories about the bride and groom and then witnessed a wonderful, emotional marriage played out live on-air.

From our vantage point in the studio, it was like watching a wonderful movie unfold. Nothing funny or crazy happened, but listeners were glued to their radio all morning. And so was I.

Sometimes I can't believe what I get do at work.

FORE!

Years ago when I worked in Vancouver, I was asked to help out with the Boys and Girls Club Golf tournament. I thought 'help out' meant emceeing the gala afterwards, or racing around the course in a golf cart. I was wrong.

'Help out' in this case meant actually playing in the tournament.

I've never golfed in my life, but how hard could it be? All I had to do was whack a little ball around a field in the beautiful sunshine, socialize and drink beer, right?

Wrong. I was placed on a team with three middle-aged men who spend all their free time (you guessed it) golfing. I went 18 holes in the blazing sun and I was horrible. I could not hit that stupid ball if my life depended on it.

And it didn't help that the men on my team kept laughing behind my back. I later found out they weren't laughing at my golf swing. Being ignorant in the ways of golf, I was wearing low-rise pants and showing plumber butt every time I bent over.

Despite all this, a golf angel was looking down on me. When I finally made contact with the ball, I hit it so far I had the second longest drive for a lady.

For the rest of the afternoon, my golf team and I bonded. We laughed. We drank beer. And they schooled me on what to wear on the golf course.

Besides low rise pants and pink underwear.

SUE STEWART

VARIETY 104 FM CORNWALL, ONTARIO
WWW.VARIETY104.COM

After graduating with honors and the Marian Wall Award from Loyalist College in Belleville, Sue Stewart started her radio career at 101.5 MoreFm in Huntsville, Ontario in 1997. A year later Sue gave birth to her son Ryan and wanting to raise him closer to home, she switched to a part time gig in Cornwall.

After several promotions, Sue is now co-host of the Variety 104 morning show in the beautiful Seaway Valley. She's a fun loving, enthusiastic gal with a love for poutine & Labbatt Sterling (to balance out her carb intake, of course!)

When Sue is not on-air she spends a lot of time with friends, working on her house, golfing, and hanging with her best bud, her son Ryan. As a single parent, Sue is treasuring this time with Ryan, but eventually wants to spread her wings in the media world, and give tv a shot.

Sue's major career highlight has been meeting Tim McGraw (twice), and she'd still like to meet Oprah. And if radio doesn't work out Sue says she'd love to snag Mary Hart's job, but figures she'd probably end up with Jerry Springer's instead!

"IS THIS THING ON?"

One of the worst things *ever* is getting up and going to work on a freezing cold December morning, especially if you're heading to a crowded local mall during the Christmas shopping season. It's even worse if you held the title of "Partying Superwoman" the night before. Out frolicking until 2am with a beverage in hand at all times. That was me a few years ago.

I had slept through my alarm and ended up scrambling around in the dark getting ready for a day I really didn't want to face. I was ready in minutes, but still groggy as I dragged my butt out the door.

My live broadcast started one hour before the mall opened. The idea was to get shoppers out early "so you don't miss out on the great deals". But when I reached the mall I found two Brinks truck drivers by my remote set up. They wouldn't let me near it until they were finished with their 'official' money duties.

If you're keeping score at home, here's the playback: I had been drinking and partying the night before; I was tired, hung over and quite grumpy. I slept through my alarm, busted my hump to get to work on time, and now I can't get near my radio booth and have to use a payphone to call the station.

I finally got a hold of Jack, the new guy at the station, who asked me how things were going. If I remember correctly, the conversation went something like this...

Jack: "Hey Sue, how are you this morning?"

Sue: "Whadaya think? I'd rather be in bed right now, Jack."

Jack: "Anything exciting going on down there?"

Sue: "Well, the brinks truck guys are keeping me

from getting near my remote set up so I had to call you from a freakin' pay phone!"

Jack: "Any good deals to talk about?"

Sue: "Huh? I don't know. I'm too lazy to walk around...when are we going on the air?"

Jack: "Well actually, Sue...we're on the air right now."

Oops.

ANDREA EVERITT (SHIGEMI)

HOT 93 SASKATOON, SASKATCHEWAN
WWW.HOT93.COM

Andrea started her radio career in 2000 in her hometown of Lethbridge, Alberta. After several years, married life took Andrea to Saskatoon where she divides her time between a radio show at Hot 93 FM, and a busy home life with hubby, Tyler and daughter, Ashton.

It's really tough to narrow down the one thing Andrea loves about radio: it's a tie between listening to music for a living, and talking to musicians like Terri Clark and Emerson Drive. Andrea also admits she's part geek, and loves the technology involved in bringing a radio station to life. (She gets that from her hubby who worked for a while as a radio engineer.)

Andrea's motivation for contributing to this book came from her biggest fan, aunt Sharlene Shigemi who owned a flower shop in Taber, Alberta. Auntie Shar would round up all the aunts and send Andrea "fan mail flowers" with cute messages.

Auntie Shar was positive, strong and inspiring, but she lost her battle with breast cancer on July 9, 2005.

MY LITTLE SISTER

I have so many great stories and moments from working in the radio "biz". Some funny, some sweet, and some that I'd better not talk about!

One of my fondest memories came from working in Lethbridge at 107.7 The River. My very first day on the job, I received a call from a young girl named Danni who introduced herself and welcomed me to the station. I thought that was pretty sweet.

We clicked right off the bat and Danni became my most treasured caller. She asked me to become her "Big Sister", and over the years I saw her grow up. She'd tell me about problems with boys or at school; we'd have lunch together; she even sat in on my show.

It was a great experience. I learned a lot from Danni and when I moved away she wrote me the sweetest letter saying how special I was to her and that she'd never forget me.

Whenever I'm having a bad day I think about that part of my radio life, and I remember how very special and rewarding my 'job' is.

CHERYL BROOKS

EZ ROCK 104.9 EDMONTON, ALBERTA
WWW.EZROCK1049.COM

Cheryl started her radio career in 1986. The day after high school graduation she enrolled at WABC Broadcasting School in Saskatoon, and four months later was interning at CJVR in Melfort, Saskatchewan.

After jobs at 900 CKBI and Power 99FM in Prince Albert, Cheryl moved to Edmonton in 1992. She worked at CISN FM for almost 10 years, left the radio biz for a while, and has since returned to 104.9 EZ ROCK.

Cheryl is the morning show co-host and loves her job. It's fantastic going to work everyday and knowing you are expected to joke around, laugh and have fun.

THE SKI BUNNY

I was born and raised in Saskatchewan, so it should come as no surprise that I never learned to downhill ski. And I thought everyone at the radio station was aware of that. So when the station ski team invited me to join them at Sunshine Village in Banff I was thrilled. Of course I never thought they actually expected me to ski.

They did.

Picture my horrifying experience: I lost all sense of balance, I walloped a fellow skier in the head with my poles, and I fell at least 7 times just trying to put the skis on. Good grief. I hadn't even gotten to the top of the hill yet.

I actually had so much trouble just trying to get to the chairlift without killing myself that someone immediately signed me up for ski lessons. There were 7 other people in the class and I was by far the worst. We were all beginners, but the instructor also recognized me as a liability. He quickly separated me from the rest of the herd and passed me on to different ski teacher.

Yes. I was so bad, I was in a class by myself! All I had to do was look into the eyes of my new instructor and I could tell what he was thinking. "Great! Another afternoon babysitting someone on the bunny hill."

To his credit he was very professional. And I was honest with him right from the start, explaining my skiing genes were severely disabled. There was absolutely no hope for me. I couldn't even walk with these stupid boards strapped to my feet!

I was also getting paranoid. The rest of the skiers on the bunny hill were whizzing by me, shooting pathetic looks in my direction. 6 year olds can be really mean!

My ski instructor turned out to be a great guy. Very patient. He was determined to teach me something, but to tell you the truth I just wasn't into it. All I wanted to do was lose those pesky skis and hit the lounge.

What happened next could not have been planned out better ... I was inching my way sideways to get away from the traffic, and suddenly started sliding down the hill. Backwards! I know it was just the bunny hill, but it could have been a double diamond mountain run, for all

I cared. I was freaked out!

Of course I panicked! Was I picking up speed? OHMYGOD!

I reached out desperately and grabbed my instructor's jacket. I was so frantic I actually whacked him in the head a few times before I actually got a hold of his jacket.

As I continued my backwards drop, I managed to slide over the top of his skis. Neither of us could move. Then I fell over sideways, taking him out in the process.

Lying together in a tangled heap in the snow he looked at me, shook his head and groaned. "Now you're making us both look bad." He suggested we call it a day. Finally. Enough of this hell.

As I slowly inched my way back to the chalet, a teenage snowboarder smacked me from behind.

I haven't looked at a pair of skis since.

TARA HOLMES

98.3 CIFM KAMLOOPS, BC
WWW.98.3CIFM.COM

40 year old Tara Holmes has spent half her life in radio. She has worked in the BC Kootenays, the Fraser Valley and Australia. Tara has since returned to Canada and her radio home for the past 10 years has been 98.3 FM in Kamloops, BC.

Tara loves her job for many reasons, mostly because she doesn't have to act her age. Radio highlights over the past few years include participating in a cattle drive, a banjo playing contest, and a bodybuilding competition.

VERY FANNY... I MEAN, FUNNY

About fifteen years ago I was on the air at radio station 4CC in Gladstone, Queensland, Australia. Being on the air in a different country was an amazing experience and I didn't anticipate there to be any language barriers. After all they spoke English.

At the time there were some great concerts in the area, including Cher. She was fantastic on stage, but her slinky stage outfit left nothing to the imagination.

The day after the concert I mentioned the tattoos that Cher had on her fanny. Every single one of my studio phones lit up immediately.

Minutes later, the boss came running into the studio and asked what I had just said on air. I explained that I was talking about Cher's skimpy outfit. And the fact that you could SEE the tattoos on her rear end.

He jumped in right away asking, "Did you say rear end? Or fanny?" I honestly couldn't remember, but who really cared?

Then he explained there most certainly WAS a difference. In Australia (as well as England) the word fanny is not your bum. Boy and girls have bums, but a fanny… well only women have that and it's NOT your bum.

I was the only person in that Australian town with an accent. And everyone knew I was the one that said 'that bad word' on the radio.

I actually thought it was quite fanny.

Oops.

I mean FUNNY!

JOY METCALFE

CKNW VANCOUVER, BC
WWW.CKNW.COM

Joy has been a broadcast journalist since 1972, covering the social scene on the west coast. Her radio home is CKNW in Vancouver. For the past 13 years Joy's Journal has been featured twice daily on CKNW, and Joy now does a weekly Journal at www.cknw.com.

Joy is also a columnist and photographer for the publications BC Restaurant News and Vancouver Lifestyles.

GO HAVE ONE

I was absolutely delighted when I was asked to contribute to this book. I have been covering the west coast social scene for so long, and doing Joy's Journal twice-a-day on CKNW radio for almost 14 years. I have so many funny stories to tell. And proceeds from this book are going to breast cancer research, so I was more than happy to help out.

Then everything changed.

A few days after I submitted my stories I went for my annual mammogram. It was January 19th, 2006. I'll never forget that date because the next morning my doctor's nurse called to say that they had found something suspicious.

The phrase 'something suspicious' can be gut-wrenching. The moment I heard it, my peaceful, contented world, sharply tilted. I remember thinking that they had to be wrong - there had to be a mix-up. Unfortunately after several more mammograms and ultrasounds, my surgeon agreed with the diagnosis and suggested a lumpectomy.

He operated on February 28th and after further testing, he confirmed that it was a small, non-aggressive cancer and that he had removed it completely. One month later on March 28th he operated again, this time removing several lymph nodes.

Despite all the fear and trauma and overwhelming desire to just break down and cry during those three terrible months, I kept repeating to myself "keep it together, keep it together". If you can pretend that it's not that bad, that everything's going to be okay, everyone else in your life will believe it too.

After Dr. Creedon reported that the lymph nodes were fine and the cancer hadn't spread, the horrible sick feeling in the pit of my stomach was replaced by an amazing sense of euphoria and freedom.

I wasn't going to die. I was going to be able to grow old with my husband, my six kids, six grandkids and little Joseph, our first great-grandchild.

It was thanks to that mammogram.

I have been given a second chance at life and I am so happy and so grateful. And so lucky! I'm currently in the midst of 16 consecutive radiation treatments at the BC Cancer Clinic. Compared to what I've been through so far, they're a breeze.

In BC, the mammogram slogan for 2006 is Go Have One. Do it today. Please.

It could save your life.

JODI HUGHES

CJAY 92 CALGARY, ALBERTA
WWW.CJAY92.COM

Jodi Hughes could tune in a radio station before she could walk. Her dad (Jimmy Hughes) was part of the Calgary radio scene for years, and she actually grew up watching him work at CFAC.

Jodi knew radio was her destiny, and in 1990 she got a job in the CFAC promotions department. Her dream was to be behind the microphone, which meant moving to stations in Drumheller, Edmonton and Prince George. With some experience under her belt Jodi finally returned to Calgary as co-host of the morning show at CJAY 92.

According to Jodi: "Radio is very immediate & so personal. People get to know you FAST, so you learn how to just be a real person and hopefully how to laugh at your flaws. In my case I've had LOTS to laugh at!"

COLBY & SIMBA

Sounds like a fancy hair salon, but those are actually the names of my 2 dogs. Colby is my five year old Border Collie/Kuvasz who is ALWAYS getting into trouble. And Simba is my eleven year old Samoyed. He actually used to be my brother's dog. I was asked to dog-sit for three weeks when my brother went to Holland. (That was eight years ago.)

Simba is quite the media star. He used to come to work with me in Edmonton, and he actually appeared on tv with me in Prince George. Or as he tells the story, I appeared with HIM on tv.

And Colby has just been constant fun. I've talked about Colby on the air so much, I've had offers from dog trainers and obedience teachers who realize we could use some help. If you've ever heard me on the air, you know my boy Colby ate an entire box of tampons, destroyed my kitchen table and chairs, then munched through a cordless phone and a couple feather pillows for dessert!

Our listeners know all about my life as a mom of 2 dogs. They know that my boys send Christmas cards, and they believe in 'Santa Paws'. They sleep on the bed and get more space than my boyfriend does. And Colby has developed the bad habit of sitting on my shoulder when I watch tv. (At a hundred pounds that isn't really the most convenient place for him to sit.)

PRINCE GEORGE TO THE RESCUE

When I was on air in Prince George I set up a regular weekly feature with my pal, Jeanine, from the local Humane Society. She would join us on air with an animal that needed a 'forever home'.

Every week I would say, "Jeanine, if this little guy doesn't find a home, let me know and I'll take him." Thank goodness she didn't have the heart to turn my house into Noah's Ark, because she never took me up on the offer.

BUT one Friday morning Jeanine called me in tears. She explained that the shelter was overflowing with dogs. They only had 24 cages, but more than 50 strays had been brought in.

Someone would be given the unthinkable task of walking up and down the corridor and randomly picking out pups to go to Doggie Heaven. Not because they were bad or hard to handle or unlovable. There was just no room for them. Of course, the girls could not bring themselves to do that. So Jeanine called me to ask if we could get this on the air and try find homes for these pups. We had until 5 pm.

We told the story on air right away, and talked about it all day. I was in tears, and all the while I'm trying to think of how in the world I am going to tell my 2 dogs that they now have 25 new brothers and sisters.

What a blessing that all this happened in a community like Prince George.

At 4:45, Jeanine called me in tears again but with good news. Over 30 dogs had been adopted and not one of them would have to leave our world too early.

What an awesome, emotional day.

I LOVE radio!

TISH ICETON

98.1 CHFI FM TORONTO, ONTARIO
WWW.CHFI.COM

Tish Iceton is on-air at 98.1 CFHI in Toronto. She has unpacked her suitcase so many times it's difficult to know where "home" is. Originally from Purcell's Cove, just outside of Halifax, Tish remembers listening to the radio late at night under the blankets. She has always loved music, going back to record albums. In fact, growing up Tish was that one kid in the neighbourhood with all the 45's. (Only 20 cents each back then!)

Tish counts broadcasting as only one of her many incarnations, but the one she has pursued the longest. Over 25 years, she has enjoyed a radio career working on both coasts and spots in-between, and she's had the privilege of working with some of the most talented broadcasters in the country.

A GOOD HOMECOOKED MEAL

Summer 1998. THE hottest new boy band, N'Sync, is coming to town. Everyone is saying they're the next Backstreet Boys! Young girls scream and follow them around shamelessly, and everyone is talking about the concert.

Tickets had been sold out for weeks and I was going to interview them. My daughter would have the chance to meet them. We were both quite excited!

N'Sync concert day finally arrives and all the boys show up for the interview - JC, Joey, Lance, Justin and Chris. They are such nice young men. Very polite, funny, pleasant and eager to please.

The boys from N'Sync posed for numerous pictures with my daughter and her friend. And as they signed autographs, I thought to myself how hard it would be for these young fellows to be so far away from home. They must really miss their parents.

The boys were all so darn sweet that my motherly instincts kicked in. I decided to invite them to come out to our cottage after the show. We could have a nice home cooked dinner and a huge bonfire.

I wasn't sure what time their curfew was but maybe we could roast some marshmallows. And maybe N'Sync would like to join my family in a fun campfire sing-along!

Are you laughing yet? Embarrassed for me? Not only did I invite N'Sync out to the cottage, I gave both their tour bus driver and their road manager very detailed directions. I'm a mother – it's what I do!

I honestly expected the boys to hop on that bus and make their way out to the lake immediately after the concert. I had tons of food prepared, the sauna was all fired up and I was going to make sure these young boys were taken care of. Just like their moms would want them to be.

How naive! I found out the next day that after the show they had gone to the seediest bar in town to drink and chase women.

This story makes me laugh no matter how many times I tell it!

SUSAN SIERRA

CLEAR FM VANCOUVER, BC
WWW.1049CLEARFM.COM

Susan started in radio at age 15 in small town, BC. Her first big on air "break" came a few years later in 1989. She was hired at CISL 650 in Vancouver for a swing shift, which means a mix of evening shows, overnights and weekend shifts.

At age 18, most of the music on this oldies station was older than Susan, but she was just excited to be living in the big city and working in radio. That excitement actually carried over into Susan's personal life... and that's where her story starts.

SUNDAY MORNING AFTER

It was early one Sunday morning, about 3am. I was doing what most other 18 year old girls do at that age: partying with my friends, dancing on tables, and pushing out of my mind the fact that I had to be up at 4:30 to do the early morning shift on-air.

I managed to catch a half hour nap before beginning what would soon be the longest and most memorable day of my life.

I was still groggy when I dragged my butt into the station for my 6 am shift. With the help of two pots of coffee I just barely made it through the first 90 minutes of music until 7:30. That's when the Lutheran Hour began, a pre-recorded show on reel to reel. Usually I was indifferent about that particular segment, but today I was so relieved I could sit back and relax for half an hour.

We had a comfy leather couch in the radio station lounge just down the hall, and that morning it was almost screaming out my name. "Okay," I thought. "I'm gonna lay down and rest. But just for a couple of minutes."

Remember, I was 18 at the time. Within seconds I was fast asleep. I woke up rather startled at 8:45. Forty five minutes after the Lutheran hour ended. Forty five minutes of dead air. OHMYGOSH!

I hurled myself off the couch and down the hall, running faster than I've ever ran, to the control room. The news guy was outside pounding on the window to get in. I scrambled to put some music on, realizing that all my phone lines were ringing and I had missed at least 10 minutes of commercials.

Moments later my boss arrived (it was Sunday so it must be serious). His face was so red I thought he would burst. And he did. He fired me on the spot.

My short-lived career flashed before my eyes.

I took a few minutes to compose myself, fix my bed-head, and wipe the sleep drool from my cheek. And attempt to convince my boss to give me another chance. He did, thank goodness.

That was a good lesson for me early in my career. And to this day I've saved the table dancing for my days off.

CARA GRAHAM

THE FAN 590 680 NEWS TORONTO, ONTARIO
WWW.FAN590.COM WWW.680NEWS.COM

Cara was lucky enough to start her radio career in Canada's largest radio market, Toronto. She has worked at almost every station in the city: Q107, Talk 640, EZ Rock , The Fan 590, Kiss Fm, Chfi, 680 NEWS and Jack FM. Cara has held gigs as an entertainment lifestyles reporter, co-host, promotions coordinator and traffic reporter.

Off the air,Cara runs her own event planning and promotions/ publicity company and has acted in a number of commercials. She has also produced a popular event in Toronto for two years: "The Starlight Soul Connection" Bachelor Bachelorette auction, a hugely successful fundraiser for the Starlight Children's Foundation.

According to Cara: "It's funny how at first you're so excited about being on the radio. It's such a big deal when you get your first on-air gig, but as the years go by it just becomes your job. Then from time to time, listeners and fans will remind you how amazing it is to have a job like this."

MY FIRST GIG

Most announcers start their careers doing the overnight show at a teeny little radio station in SmallTown, Canada. But I got really lucky with my first radio gig.

A year after graduating from Humber College, I was working several different jobs. Unfortunately none of them were in radio.

I was driving home from my office temp job and listening to Q107. The DJ on-air at the time was Howard Cogan (Hungry Man Cogan) and my ears went on full alert when I heard him mention that Q107 was looking for a number babe. A number babe? Are you kidding – I was great at that! A number babe? I was *born* to be a number babe. (Okay, I didn't really know what a number babe was, but if it meant getting my foot in the door at Toronto's coolest rock station, I'm sure I could handle it.)

Hungry Man asked listeners to call in and describe why they should be the new number babe. Of course, I had to give it a shot. The receptionist sent my call straight to Hungry Man's voicemail. Not sure if that was a good sign, but I left a message anyway.

The next day I hadn't heard anything so I decided to drop by the station. It must have been fate. As I was pulling into the parking lot *I heard my own voice on the air.* Hungry Man was playing my voicemail and asking callers what they thought.

I parked my car, walked into the station and identified myself. Then things got crazy. They immediately whisked me upstairs to the studio. In a whirlwind I was thrown a pair of head phones, introduced to 'Hungry Man', and told, "okay we're coming up, turn your mic on." HUH?

There I was, a year out of radio school and auditioning *live on air* at a Toronto station.

And I got the job! It was such a great experience and I had so much fun. We would joke around a lot and talk about the latest entertainment stories. And my biggest job duty was counting down the top 6 songs at 6, in my sexy radio number babe voice. Hence the title, "number babe"!

Those chance auditions rarely happen in radio, but I got lucky and got my foot in the door. I've loved radio ever since!

NAME DROPPING

Throughout my career I've met lots of high profile celebrities including: Lenny Kravitz, Gordon Lightfoot, Our Lady Peace, Julian Lennon, Jann Arden, Blondie, Sarah McLachlan, Blue Rodeo, Sound Garden, Randy Bachman, David Crosby, Hulk Hogan and numerous athletes and politicians.

Here are a few 'star' anecdotes:

Gene Simmons

I met Gene while he was in town promoting his tell-all biography "KISS and Make-up". As soon as he walked into the room you could feel how huge his personality was. He was very laid back and soft spoken and I love that he was willing to sit and chat for a while. Of course I had to ask if he would show me that famous tongue of his. "Sure", he slyly responded. "Only if you show me yours first!" He reached over touched my hand and added, "it better be good sexy!" Let's just say he was pleasantly surprised by what I produced, and asked if there was any way we could be related. For a huge rock star he was a pretty genuine guy. My friends still get a kick out of this story.

Lenny Kravitz

I've always been a huge fan of Lenny Kravitz. I've seen him in concert several times so I was really excited to meet him. But here's a surprise: my lovely Lenny likes to go 'au natural' when it comes to deodorant. I met him briefly while working at Q107 and all I really remember is his really big sunglasses, his entourage of people and his scent, which lingered on my shoulder long after he left the building. Still, it was very cool to have Lenny Kravitz wrap his arm around you and call you "doll".

Don Cherry

Love, love, love him! Working at the FAN 590 I've had the chance to meet so many athletes and sports personalities but Don Cherry was the best. Not only does he have his own special flare for fashion, (I love the loud suits he wears on Hockey night in Canada.) He is also one of the few sports personalities left who has no fear when it comes to truly speaking his mind. I'm tired of listening to guys who get paid big bucks to just sit on the fence instead of having a firm opinion. Not only is Cherry a truly proud Canadian, if you ever meet him in person, ladies, you'll see he's quite handsome. Oh yeah and one more thing: unlike Lenny Kravitz, Don Cherry always smells very good.

LISA RENDALL

C95 FM SASKATOON, SASKATCHEWAN
WWW.C95.COM

Lisa Rendall started her radio career in Estevan, Saskatchewan in 1984. From there it was on to stations in Regina, Toronto and finally the morning show at C95 in Saskatoon.

In July of 2000 at the age of 35, Lisa was diagnosed with metastatic breast cancer after a vertebra in her neck collapsed. It was scary and painful. And it was life altering.

Lisa's personal mission now is to raise as much money as possible for breast cancer research. Six years after she was first diagnosed, she continues to create awareness through fundraising events like the C95 Radio Marathon and the Lisa Rendall Golf Classic. Since July of 2000, the C95 Radio Marathon has raised over $800,000 dollars for breast cancer research; and the Lisa Rendall Golf Classic has contributed $121,500 to the C95 Radio Marathon.

Lisa's positive attitude and sense of humour have helped her live and thrive with cancer. She is still taking treatment and her cancer remains stable, 6 years after diagnosis.

RADIO PERKS

I've had the privilege of meeting a lot of celebrities over the years. It's one of the great perks of being a radio announcer, especially when you find yourself face to face with someone you've always admired.

Almost every celebrity I've met has been exactly what I imagined, but there have been some surprises. And disappointments.

In 1989 I found myself backstage, waiting to meet Gordon Lightfoot after his concert in Regina. My husband and I were escorting some radio contest winners, and the fact that the fan meeting was after the concert was highly unusual. *(Insider Secret #1: Stars usually hold the fan 'meet and greet' BEFORE the concert, to limit the time you have with them. I.e. "It was nice to meet you, but I have to get ready for my performance. Enjoy the show!")*

The 'meet and greet' is much like a cattle call. Everyone lines up, the star walks in and you are quickly escorted to him/her for a 'smile and a snapshot'. Then it's on to the next person.

We were warned beforehand that Gordon Lightfoot was not a talkative man. Hello, handshake, autograph, picture, and out the door. To my surprise, we received the exact opposite reaction. Gordon Lightfoot was in the mood to visit that night. We actually sat down to chat. *(Insider Secret #2: Fans never, EVER sit down during a celebrity 'meet and greet'. It's usually held in a stadium hallway, or a room backstage. With no chairs. Don't want to get too comfy.)*

Myself, my hubby and our radio listeners were all entranced as the legendary Gordon Lightfoot shared many personal stories of his life. It was incredibly cool to hear about the music business from a real Canadian icon. Mr. Lightfoot was charming, candid and real.

It was an awesome moment and our radio contest winners were thrilled.

Who am I kidding? So was I!

"HELLO. I'M JOHNNY CASH"

One of the highlights of my star encounters occurred while I was working at CJWW in Saskatoon. I literally begged to be the announcer to escort a contest winner backstage to meet Johnny Cash, one of THE great legends of country music. My parents were huge Cash fans when I was growing up, and like millions of others I loved his music too.

I was as excited as our contest winners (maybe even a teeny bit more) as we paced backstage, anxiously awaiting The Man In Black.

No word of a lie, goose bumps covered my entire body when I first heard his deep, booming voice.

"Hello…I'm Johnny Cash". You can almost hear it, can't you?

The legendary 'Man In Black' had an amazing presence, almost a visible aura that surrounded him. This may sound strange, but you could actually feel how special he was just by being in the same room.

It was electric and emotional. I had tears in my eyes the entire time.

"Hello…I'm Johnny Cash".

ALWAYS WEAR NICE UNDERWEAR

I was working at CISS FM in Toronto and for a photo shoot we all had to wear shirts with our radio station logo. I wasn't wearing a CISS shirt, so I went to the promo department to snag one. This all happened while I was on air, so I decided to slip on my new t-shirt in the control room. No big deal since I was alone.

In fact, I actually stood with my butt against the control room door so nobody could walk in and see me with my top off. I stripped off my shirt, did my little happy dance, put on the new t-shirt and slid my butt away from the control room door. I was dressed. No need for the "Butt Barricade".

As I spun around to get back to my microphone, I found myself staring through the control room window. Directly into the arched eyebrows and huge smirk of radio personality Cliff Dumas. Cliff is not only a famous Toronto radio announcer. He is also the voice of CMT, Country Music Television. Cliff had been sitting in the news booth, working on something for his show. He saw the whole thing.

And I hadn't even noticed him. I was so busy barricading the door closed with my butt that I forgot we had THREE other booths that looked directly into the control room. Anyone could have been in the news, traffic or sports booth to witness it all. My shirt off. My happy dance. My butt holding the door closed. It just happened to be our morning man, Cliff.

Here's the crazy thing. I wasn't at all embarrassed that he saw me change my shirt. I was humiliated because I was wearing a really ugly bra! The one day I take my shirt off and someone sees, I happen to be wearing my one ugly, fraying ratty bra!

MY CAREER ENDS... THE BATTLE BEGINS

July 20, 2000 was the day my life changed forever. I was 35 years old and had just been diagnosed with metastatic breast cancer. Metastatic means that the cancer has spread to other areas of my body.

I'd had various aches and pains for years after escaping two separate accidents: one in a car, the other with a Clydesdale at a media event. In January of 2000, mysterious and troublesome pain started to plague me. First in my lower back, then my ribs, shoulders and neck.

What turned out to be my last day on the job was a live broadcast to celebrate the summer exhibition. My neck pain was so severe I was barely hanging on, trying to finish the show without breaking down in tears. There were a lot of listeners visiting our broadcast booth, and it was one of my worst radio memories ever. I could barely hold my head up, never mind smile and make small talk.

I got through that final show, but by the next week I was confined to my bed, barely able to use the washroom or feed myself. After several doctor visits I was informed I had a collapsed vertebra in my neck and I should get to the emergency room at Saskatoon City Hospital immediately.

My husband took me to emergency and after what felt like a million tests I received the bad news. I had breast cancer, which had spread to numerous areas of my body, including my spine, ribs, liver, and the vertebra in my neck. At that point, my husband had to make the most difficult phone calls of his life ... to my parents, my boss and several close friends.

I didn't realize how serious my condition was until the ambulance attendants came to take me to Royal University Hospital. They wouldn't let me get out of bed.

They put me on a backboard, sandbagged either side of my head, and drove very carefully to emergency, where I heard incredulous whispers outside the curtains. "She actually walked into emergency?"

I was more shaken when my three neurosurgeons told me they needed to put me in a halo. The term may not sound familiar, but I'm sure you've seen one before. A halo is a metal contraption that is placed over your head, neck and shoulders, to stabilize you in ONE position. You can't turn your neck and you have to turn your entire body if you want to see something. It's attached to your head with metal pins that pierce the skin and rest on the skull where there are no nerve endings. Sound awful? It was.

As soon as my halo was on I felt like an infant. I could not move on my own. I was stranded in a hospital bed, dependent on the nurses or my husband to move and bathe me.

I had non-stop visits from co-workers, family members and friends. At this point we had not made any announcements on the radio about what was happening. The radio station listeners had only been told I was away. But so many friends and co-workers were coming to see me that the hospital moved me to the biggest room on the ward.

People told me later that they would be on their way to see me, filled with worry, only to hear laughter coming out of my hospital room. My radio co-hosts Rob Suski and Rambling Dave Scharf even put fresh nail polish on my toenails.

There was only one time through all of this when I remember being scared out of my mind. I was on a stretcher outside the operating room when the anaesthesiologist told me I would have to be awake for him to intubate me.

Normally for this surgery, a patient is put under anaesthesia before the breathing tube is inserted into their throat. Because I was in the halo, my neck could not bend and I would need to be awake for the intubation.

I immediately started to panic, telling him there was no way I could swallow that tube. As I lay there crying he assured me he would administer a drug to help me through the process. I wouldn't panic or choke to death. I wouldn't remember anything.

He won my trust and he was right. The only thing I remember from the operating room was waking up and swearing at the doctor because the halo was still on. I really hated that halo.

The cancer had eaten away my neck vertebrae and the surgery on my neck was not an easy procedure, but it had to be done. I won't go into details but I will tell you that a titanium plate was fixed inside my throat, to stabilize my neck.

After my neck was sewn up, the next surgical team came in to perform a lumpectomy. The lump in my breast had to be removed so the oncologists would know how to fight the cancer. There are over 200 different kinds of cancer, andit wasimperative that the pathologists had enough tissue to learn all they could about my cancer.

The surgery went as planned, but there was one problem. The surgeons knew my voice was my livelihood and assured me they would be as gentle as possible during the surgery. Unfortunatelyin the end I was left with a paralysed vocal cord. I saw an ear, nose and throat specialist who told me there was a 50-50 chance of my voice returning. I had to be taught how to swallow again and got pneumonia after the surgery, which meant I needed large amounts of antibiotics.

My husband became my caregiver when I went home, and he definitely upheld our marriage vows of 'in sickness and in health, for better or worse'. He gave me I.V. antibiotics three times a day, cleaned the four halo pins in my head, and washed under my halo vest twice a day. I joked that he hadn't touched my breasts that many times in our 11 years of marriage!

For three months, I wasn't allowed to shower because I was still wearing the halo. It took 2 or 3 people to wash my hair over the kitchen sink with the vegetable sprayer.

My physiotherapist taught me how to function with a halo. I had to get out of bed with the help of a pole that went from floor to ceiling by my bed, and was able to use the washroom with the help of a commode.

And all this time I kept wondering, "what about the cancer?"

In September I was strong enough for chemotherapy. There were many side effects but the one that was the hardest to deal with was what happened to my fingernails. Every finger looked and felt like it had been pounded by a hammer and had a huge build-up of blood underneath. Two of them had to be drained at the doctor's office, and I wore a bandage on every finger for over six months after my treatment ended.

I bought surgical gloves by the box and what must have added up to cases of bandages. I couldn't prepare food with bandaged fingers and I had to tape the gloves onto my hands when I showered.

I finished my chemotherapy in February of 2001 and the cancer has remained stable since then. I still have cancer tumours throughout my body, but they have not grown and that is the best we can hope for.

I am on Long Term Disability and have not returned

to work but I have made it my mission to raise as much money as possible for breast cancer research.

Every year in October (breast cancer awareness month) we hold the C95 Radio Marathon. Our wonderful C95 announcers broadcast live from a Saskatoon mall for 35 hours straight, and I love being back on the air during the marathon.

From 2000 to 2005 we raised over $800,000 for breast cancer research at the Saskatchewan Cancer Agency. I also hold a golf tournament called the Lisa Rendall Golf Classic every summer with all proceeds going to the C95 Radio Marathon. In the first 5 years the tournament raised $121,500.

The support from our radiolisteners has been overwhelming. I actually have a binder full of emails and a box full of cards and letters from listeners. If I ever need a boost I can go read some of the wonderful things people wrote to me.

Talking about my diagnosis helped me cope with it, and the more you talk about it the easier it gets. When I was first diagnosed I was told the median survival rate for someone with cancer as widespread as mine was 2.5 years. My God. Two and a half years. Left to live. And do everything I needto do.

But six years later my cancer is still stable. I have three different treatments every month and I continue to raise money for breast cancer research any way I can. It's my way of fighting this disease and trying to find a cure. Even if it's too late for me, it will benefit others who follow in my footsteps.

I'm lucky enough to have lived many of my dreams through my radio career. If you have a dream, don't wait. Go for it now! The phrase "life is too short" has a whole new meaning for me. I hope you embrace that.

On behalf of all breast cancer survivors, those who have lost their lives and those who are fighting right now, THANK YOU.

Thank you for buying this book to raise money for breast cancer research. It means SO much I can't sufficiently explain it in words.

Index of Contributors

ISBN 141209637-5

9 781412 096379